CHURCH LIFE IN NORWAY
1800-1950

CHURCH
IN NORWAY

by EINAR MOLLAND
translated by HARRIS KAASA

AUGSBURG PUBLISHING HOUSE

LIFE
1800-1950

CHURCH LIFE IN NORWAY
1800—1950
© Augsburg Publishing House 1957

Library of Congress Catalog Card No. 57-6474

Printed and Manufactured in the United States of America
by Augsburg Publishing House, Minneapolis 15, Minnesota

PREFACE

Only an exceptional church historian could in one hundred pages flash before us one hundred fifty stormy years of church history as vividly as Professor Molland does in this little book

From the fervent pietism of Hauge which launched the nineteenth century, through the pietistic orthodoxy of Johnson and Caspari, to the wartime reign of militant churchman Berggrav, the author weaves a fascinating tale of the growth of a great national church, the Church of Norway.

By giving us this work in excellent translation, Mr. Kaasa has offered to English-speaking Christendom an intimate glimpse of a sturdy branch of the world church.

Readers will quickly recognize the relevance of this compactly written church history to the life of the church today. Here they will discover the rich heritage—theological, religious, and cultural—which underlies the virile section of English-speaking Lutheranism that first took root in the fjords and mountains of Norway. The relevance of this book to American church life will readily become apparent to the alert reader.

The pietism of Hans Nielsen Hauge is the Norwegian edition of the great movement in England and America known as Puritanism. The Orthodoxy of the latter 19th century in Norway is the living Orthodoxy of the Reformation which the two great scholars, Johnson and Caspari, injected into the University and thus into the Norwegian clergy.

The age of Berggrav and Hallesby projects the Norwegian church on the world scene in heroic proportions. When the war drove the Norwegian government of Church and State to London, Anglican Christendom was compelled to feel the power of the exiled church. It had now come of age and had risen to leadership in the world family of churches.

This book presents the Church of Norway, its theology and life, as a living force in Christendom.

HERMAN A. PREUS, PH.D.

Professor of New Testament, Symbolics, and Liturgics, Luther Theological Seminary St. Paul, Minnesota

Contents

Chapter One

The Hauge Awakening
Reconstruction of Church Life
Beginnings of Grundtvigianism

In the history of Norway—both in the political and economic history and in the spiritual history—there are two periods which possess a certain glory: The High Middle Ages and the 19th Century. The centuries which lie between them are not, for the Norwegian mind, surrounded with any particular glory. Henrik Wergeland once said that the Norway of the Middle Ages and the Norway of his age fit together like the two broken halves of a gold ring, once the solder that binds them together is removed. This view of Norway's history has gradually been corrected by historical research. The centuries between are not so dark and destitute as we have often thought, and there is far more continuity in the history of Norway than Wergeland's words expressed.

However, despite this very necessary correction, the prevailing historical interpretation is correct

1

in looking upon the 19th Century as a time of awakening of story-book proportions and a marvelous period of expansion on all fronts: a reawakened political life after centuries of slumber, a large-scale economic expansion, an enormous improvement in means of transportation, coupled with a rapidly growing national unity, a rise in standard of living, a sharp increase in popular education, the progressive growth of Norwegian learning (made possible by the founding of Oslo University in 1811, until quite recently Norway's only university), a literary "golden age" which began with Henrik Wergeland and continued until Sigrid Undset, and also a reawakened *religious* life. In all fields we see revolutionary developments and an unfolding of life which forms a sharp contrast with the preceding centuries.

The development of Norwegian church history in the nineteenth century, like that in the rest of Western Europe in this period, is marked by awakening movements which gradually consolidate themselves into organized Christian work on a voluntary basis. At the same time, a partial disintegration of the old state-church system takes place. The secularization of society begins in earnest in the second half of the century; a battle for the Christian faith emerges. The age is also characterized by intra-church tensions and struggles between different tendencies: high-churchly vs. low-churchly, pietistic vs. culturally minded, liberal vs. conservative.

Norway's first great awakening heralds the beginning of the century. Hans Nielsen Hauge awakened large segments of the Norwegian people to a personal Christianity. He called to life slumbering powers in many spheres of life. His work had an impact on political life through the rise of the small farmers, and also on economic and social life. First and foremost, however, it is the church life which bears his stamp. It was he who set in motion the laymen's activity so characteristic of Norwegian church history in the nineteenth and twentieth centuries, the work which has given Norwegian church life its mark of distinction today.

To understand the developments that follow, we must first dwell briefly upon Hauge's life.

Hans Nielsen Hauge was born in 1771, at the farm called Hauge in Tune parish, Østfold. His parents were pious and serious farmer-folk. The devotional books in use in their home give evidence of a deep piety: Luther's *Catechism* and *House Postil*, Erik Pontoppidan's Explanation of the Catechism, *Truth Unto Godliness,* and his devotional book *Mirror of Faith,* and books by

Johan Arndt, J. D. Jersin, and Henrich Müller. Luther and Lutheran pietists and pre-pietists provided the family's spiritual food.

As a child, Hauge was brooding and melancholy, early taken up with religious problems. When, in his thirteenth year, he nearly drowned, his soul was terrified by the thought that he had not loved God as he ought.

At the same time, he was in his youth exposed to a religious influence which probably had a certain positive significance for him, despite his own opinion that he only reacted strongly against it. The parish pastor in Tune was an extreme *Herrnhuter* (Moravian). His followers exhibited an emotional, sentimental piety. Hauge found them lacking in ethical seriousness. Herrnhutism in this form was repulsive to him, and this reaction marked his own interpretation of Christianity. Hauge constantly preached moral conversion and obedience to God's will. His Christianity bore the stamp of the Law. He preached the Law and Sanctification in such a way that his contemporary critic, Professor Stenersen could readily assert that Hauge was not Lutheran on this point, while Bishop Bang, Hauge's later biographer, was forced to employ no small amount of hermeneutics in order to demonstrate that his hero was Lutheran to the last jot and tittle.

On April 5, 1796, Hauge experienced his spiritual break-through. It was not a conversion from a worldly life to a godly life. Rather, it was a pious and serious Christian experiencing a sudden break-through and from that day on, possessing an assurance and a power he had not previously known. In its nature, the experience is reminiscent of John Wesley's break-through. In both instances, the experience was provoked by a Christian testimony from the past. In Hauge's case, it was an old hymn (*Jesus, I Long for Thy Blessed Communion*) which released the transformation.

Many years later, Hauge depicted this experience with a remarkable faculty for self-examination and description of spiritual experience—here, too, there is similarity between him and Wesley. The description must, as the Danish scholar Bjørn Kornerup has determined after a careful critical analysis of the sources, be authentic.

The experience was clearly ecstatic. "My soul was in that instant so uplifted to God that I was no longer conscious of myself." It brought about contrition. "I deeply regretted that I had not served God, who was very dear and in all things good." He received a blessed certitude. His soul felt "something supernatural, divine, blessed." "No one can argue me out of this." He received new light upon the Scriptures and a consciousness

that he possessed a call to witness. The latter came
to him in the form of a voice, saying: "You shall
confess My Name before men."

After that spring day in 1796, there followed
eight years of ceaseless activity as preacher, author,
organizer, and comforter to souls: then a period
of ten years, from 1804 to 1814, occupied by
Hauge's protracted imprisonment and the court
case against him; and finally, a period of ten years,
from 1814 until his death, when he no longer
travelled about.

The years 1796-1804 were years of remarkable
activity. During the first months after his awakening, Hauge did not address gatherings, but con-
centrated on personal evangelism, speaking man-
to-man. As a result, many were gripped by the
awakening. "Some became converted," he says,
"while others scoffed at me and contradicted me,
but I refuted them." Beginning in the fall of 1796,
he constantly spoke before groups. His ecclesiastical opponents were undoubtedly correct in asserting that he was an enthusiast. He himself says in
the tract *Religious Feelings:* "It was as though
there was a fire in me; I could not keep silent, especially when many people came, for it happened
that I sometimes did not really realize what I was
saying, for the feeling drove me on. And when I
afterward reflected upon whether I had spoken

aright, and, doubting, questioned the most enlightened friends about my speech, not only they,
but also my opponents admitted that I had spoken
profoundly, following Christ's teaching." On the
other hand, when he would contemplate before-
hand what he was to say, he would fail. On these
occasions, he experienced the feeling that his
preaching had been a purely human work.

We can gain only an imperfect impression of
Hauge's preaching through his writings. His books
betray a general clumsiness in style and manner
of expression, even though they show a remarkable Christian maturity and wisdom. We must re-
member that his literary training consisted in a
very deficient formal education and the reading
of old devotional literature. His works, which are
now being published in a collection complete with
critical apparatus, certainly do not give any true
picture of the fiery preacher.

Some weeks after his awakening, Hauge wrote
his first treatise, *Reflections on the World's Folly,*
and about the middle of the summer, 1796, he set
out on foot for Christiania [Oslo] to have it
printed. He published two more treatises the
same year.

From Christmas time, 1796, he began also to
preach outside his home district, first in the neigh-
boring districts, then in the nearest cities, Fredrik-

stad, Moss, Christiania, and Drammen, in an ever-widening arc. Within eight years, he travelled over most of Norway. He sailed up and down the coasts. Ashore, he walked from place to place. He has described his itinerant activities in *Travels and Important Incidents,* in which we can follow his wandering life and read his observations, not only on the religious life, but also on the peculiarities of nature, on the manners and customs of the people, and on the attitude of the local authorities toward him. These journeys must have been carried out under the most difficult circumstances, without any organization or support behind him and at first without any circle of friends to welcome him in the places to which he went. The travels were repeatedly interrupted by arrests and short jail-sentences, but as soon as he was released or transported by the police to his home, he would immediately resume his work. Consciousness of the call to preach was too strong for him to break off his activity.

Several times Hauge traversed Eastern Norway. He also visited the West coast a number of times, and here Bergen became the natural base of operations. In 1801, he took out a commercial license there, in order to establish several large business enterprises.

Early in 1803, he sailed from Bergen to Nordland with four sloops, on a combined business and preaching tour. He travelled all the way to Tromsø, visiting also the interior, and still found time that same year to visit Trøndelag, tramp over the mountains to Gudbrandsdal, and visit "most of the parishes and cities in the Christiania diocese," among them his own home village, whereupon he turned westward through Telemark and Setesdal, went down to Christiansand, then to Stavanger, proceeding to Bergen from there by sea.

Twice Hauge visited Denmark. In the spring of 1800, he sailed to Copenhagen to appeal his case and that of his friends to the King, but in Copenhagen he abandoned this plan. However, he published reprints of several of his earlier writings, a collection of meditations on the texts for the Church Year in two large volumes, and a work titled *Basis of the Christian Teaching* in two small volumes. He provided work for five printers, and one of them "worked almost steadily for four months on my account," he relates. In the summer of 1804, Hauge sailed from Bergen to Jutland, and travelled around in Jutland as far south as Christiansfeld in Southern Jutland, then through Fynen and Zeland to Copenhagen; from there he returned to Norway by ship (to Fredrikshald) and home to Tune.

One essential aspect of Hauge's message was

his accentuation of the Lutheran ethic of the call. He realized that some of the awakened would want to be free from earthly occupations, and he continually exhorted them to diligence, showing the way by his own example. Always a very hard-working man, Hauge would help with the farm work wherever people took him in, and even occupied his travel time by knitting as he walked along. On his journeys, he would instruct the farmers regarding the most effective farm implements he had seen elsewhere.

Godliness with contentment leads, in the long run, to prosperity, an observation which can be made in the history of many awakening movements. In the Hauge movement, this development occurred very rapidly, because Hauge's puritanism and his intelligent interest in things practical plus his business ability quickly steered the movement in that direction. He succeeded in setting up his friends in large economic undertakings before he was imprisoned in 1804. He saw how the "worldly-minded" had obtained for themselves wealth and prestige by applying themselves to "the most useful and profitable things, such as trade, manufacturing, and other large industry," and he sought to lift his friends to the same economic and social level. Characteristically applying Bible passages, he writes: "I believed

that we by means of more industrial and manufacturing plants, etc. . . . should seek to let our
light shine before men in good works, Matt. 5:16,
in order thereby to show a profit and thus to
possess money for giving, rather than to be obliged
to accept, Acts 20:35."

Hauge himself directed commercial enterprises
out of Bergen, bought up fishing stations, founded
trading posts, and set up his friends in business.
He persuaded one of his friends from Sørlandet
to settle down in Bergen as a merchant. For another, from Hallingdal, he purchased the large
farmstead Svanøen in Sunnfjord and set him up in
lumbering, milling, and salt refining. This place
also had dock facilities. At Eiker, near Drammen,
he established a paper mill which he turned over
to a partnership consisting of six of his friends—
a Haugeaner corporation. He was there, busily
planning new ventures, when arrested by the local
bailiff in the fall of 1804.

During all his activity, Hauge had been in constant conflict with the police authorities and with
ecclesiastical and civil officials. As early as 1796,
when he had his first encounter with the magistrates, he had learned that his meetings were contrary to the existing law, the Conventicle Act of
1741. During a devotional meeting in his home
town, he was visited by the parish pastor, the

assistant pastor, and the bailiff. They all became involved in a vehement dispute, during which both the bailiff and Hauge quoted the Conventicle Act—he had a copy of it with him and appealed to all the clauses that favored godly gatherings. The pastor and bailiff temporarily forbade the meetings. "This," relates Hauge, "shocked the common folk into asserting that the authorities sought to hinder the good and to allow the evil to go unpunished." This incident introduced a relationship which was to become characteristic of the entire awakening: the opposition between the state-church order and lay-preaching. It was also the opposition between farmer and state official. In the conflict which raged around the Conventicle Act, there was a bitter antagonism that was social in character.

During the years 1797-1804, Hauge was arrested a total of ten times in various parts of the country, for violations of the Conventicle Act and of vagrancy ordinances. The highest civil officials, the so-called *amt-men,* were less enthusiastic about prosecuting a fanatic of this sort; they found it unpleasant business. Even though his speeches were "incoherent gibberish," the awakening had good moral consequences, says one of the *amt-men.* The clergy, on the other hand, were often somewhat irritable. Hauge had several encounters

with clergymen in which he answered them clev-
erly and stubbornly. Among the bishops, meanwhile, Nordal Brun of Bergen held his protecting
hand over Hauge and his friends, even though
he was not in sympathy with their pietistic,
mournful manner. It was Brun's opinion that the
old ordinance regarding Conventicles had to be
regarded as *de facto* repealed, since freedom of
the press had been introduced in the meantime.
"If half-educated people can freely write against
God's Word for millions, then surely also uneducated people who love God's Word must be allowed to preach it freely, privately, in their way,
for a score of people."

Brun's rationalistic colleague in Christiansand,
Peder Hansen, did not share his opinion. His last
official act before leaving for Denmark to become
Bishop of Odense in 1804 was to write a report
to the Chancellery on Hauge and his followers,
in which he says that Hauge has spread much
misery among the peasants throughout the land.
The bishop besought the Chancellery "by whatever means it might find suitable, to halt an evil
which seeks both the physical and the moral ruin
of an otherwise amiable people, with tragic consequences." The Chancellery wrote to all the
bishops and *amt-men* in Norway and requested
information about Hauge's activity and proposed

remedies against "this evil." The *amt-men* and the bishops in turn wrote to their subordinates, and thus the entire ecclesiastical and legal service produced reports in 1804 regarding Hauge and his followers. On the whole, the reports were unfavorable to him. They represent him as a fanatic and a demagogue who spread superstition and fanaticism among the peasantry and who utilized religion for economic gain.

Late in October, the Chancellery issued an order for Hauge's arrest. Meanwhile, he had in fact been arrested some days earlier at Eiker for a violation of the Conventicle Act. The case against him became a long, drawn-out affair. The commission appointed to investigate the case worked slowly, assembling information from all over the country, and it was not until 1809 that the bill of indictment was formulated. By that time, Hauge had been in jail for four and one-half years. After a couple of years' confinement in milder forms, Hauge was released in the fall of 1811. The verdict was eventually handed down in December, 1813. Hauge was found guilty of repeated violations of the Conventicle Act and of making insulting remarks about the authorities. Punishment was set at two years' confinement at hard labor. Hauge appealed to the higher criminal court, and on December 23, 1814, the final sentence was pro-

nounced, reducing his punishment to a fine of one
thousand *riksdaler*.

When Hauge was released, he settled down on
a farm near Christiania. His travelling days were
over, but he maintained contact with his friends
by mail, and received visitors. He recovered eco-
nomically, and became a respected and honored
man. He frequently associated with pastors and
other officials in the capital city. He also resumed
his writing; from a literary point of view, his
best books date from this period. His earlier fire
was, however, all but quenched, and his health
had been broken by long imprisonment. He died
in 1824.

In 1821, when Hauge had a premonition that
he was about to die, he penned a *Testament to My
Friends*. In this document, he draws up the blue-
prints for the future of the Awakening and
thereby for the future of what is called the
laymen's movement in Norwegian church history. He speaks about "the congregation," the
society of the friends, the inner circle, within the
larger framework of what he calls "The Christian
Church." But he dislikes the idea of organizing a
separate church. He says that "some have called
us and regarded us as a separate sect, for which
they have no cause whatever." It is remarkable
to see how this man, who was persecuted by pas-

tors and magistrates, warns against all separatism
and exhorts his followers to loyalty toward the
church. "It is my last wish that you hereafter as
heretofore adhere exclusively to our state's religion and that you accept from the state's teachers
everything which your officials put forth; that
you attend church, receive the Sacraments, allow
the pastors to consecrate your marriages, likewise
with the sprinkling of the dust in burial, and
everything else which pertains to good order."

The laymen's movement which Hauge introduced has largely adhered to the directives he
gave in his testament. The Haugeaners and their
successors have, in the first place, been constantly
on guard against all teaching which deviates from
traditional Lutheranism. This confessionalism, a
heritage from Hauge, was further strengthened
through the Johnsonian Revival, which began
about the middle of the century. Secondly, the
lay movement did not lead to the formation of
any free church. It organized itself as a communion of friends within the state-church. No
development in the direction of a free church took
place until the 1890's, when the radical wing in
the lay movement departed from the Haugean
line and introduced private administration of the
Lord's Supper at their meetings.

When the authorities filed their reports on

Hauge in 1804, it became apparent that he had followers in almost every part of the country. The sources tell very little about their numbers—in the nature of the case, it was difficult to mark the boundaries of the movement, for it was not organized into associations. But it is certain that in several districts and cities Hauge already had hundreds of adherents at this early stage.

Hauge himself had borne the torch of the Awakening over the entire country. Yet he had co-laborers as early as the year of his conversion. Within a few years there arose a vast multitude of lay-preachers, several of whom were itinerant. Following Hauge's imprisonment in 1804, there were only a few who risked continuing as itinerant preachers, but this work began anew after 1814, and it increased sharply throughout the 20's and 30's. Many were awakened through these preachers, others through Hauge's writings, still others through reading authors like Arndt and Pontoppidan, while some were awakened through preparation for confirmation and especially through the ceremony of confirmation itself, with its solemn vow. All of these found their natural milieu among the Haugeaners.

The Hauge awakening reached out almost exclusively to one class of society, the farmers. Those of the awakened who lived in the cities were usually people who had migrated from the rural areas, and had gone into business and industry. Often, they were people who had worked themselves up into prosperous circumstances. The movement affected especially the more prosperous and alert farmers.

The awakened gathered regularly for devotional meetings, in the first generation usually around the reading aloud of a *postil* when they had no visiting preacher. Haugean piety was conventicle Christianity, yet at the same time loyal to the church. They were faithful church-goers and regularly partook of Holy Communion in the spring and fall.

God's Law was strongly emphasized in the Haugean witness and piety. Obedience toward God was a principal theme. Several Haugeaners have autobiographically described how they had sought help in books dealing with Jesus' wounds, blood, and atonement to the neglect of the struggle for faith, self-denial, and good works. It was first through Hauge's preaching of the Law that they saw the light.

In time, Haugean piety became less legalistic and more evangelical. From the mid-30's, Haugean preaching and hymnody speak more and more of God's free grace. This shift in emphasis is due especially to the lay-preacher Anders Haave who, one stormy night when he thought the end of the world had come, made a thorough self-examination and found that none of his works and not even his faith could stand up before God. He could trust only in the atonement.

The Haugeaners are the puritans of Norway. Their stand on the *adiaphora* was one of absolute rejection. Time and again, lively young men and women who had previously found joy in dancing and gaiety, music and card-playing, turned their backs on all these pleasures and denounced them. Fiddlers smashed their violins, and it was a rare exception when one of them spared his instrument and used it for playing hymns.

Ability in business was a characteristic trait among these Norwegian puritans. Several of Norway's largest mercantile firms, publishing houses, and factories were founded by them. Occasionally, we find Haugean homes in which there were also cultural interests. And several sons of Haugeans, among them Hauge's only son, later became pastors. They soon made themselves felt in politics, too. In the Constitutional Assembly of 1814, there were three Haugean farmers. The Haugeans came to form the heart of the farmer opposition bloc in the Storting. They were economizers and opponents of the official class. Their great political victory came in 1842 when they succeeded in getting the Conventicle Act repealed. Twice previously, in 1836 and 1839, a plurality in the Storting consisting of farmers and liberal officials had passed a law abolishing the Conventicle Act, but both times the King had refused his sanction. When the law was passed for the third time, the King was forced to yield and give his sanction, since according to Norwegian Constitutional law, the resolution would then have become law even without royal sanction. On the other hand, a liberal Dissenter Law was passed three years later against the votes of the Haugean farmers. They wanted freedom for their own lay-preachers, but not for the non-Lutheran sects.

For the nation as a whole, the clergy and their preaching were far more significant than Hauge and the Haugeaners.

The Norwegian clergy of about 1800 was to a great extent marked by the strong cultural interest of the Enlightenment period. These pastors have been branded by succeeding generations as rationalists. They have been very harshly and unjustly criticized by pastors and laymen of the Johnsonian orthodox-pietist school who have viewed them solely as the dark background for Hauge's radiant figure. There were indeed those who were unfit, incapable, and morally derelict, but besides these, this generation of pastors included many distinguished men. There were, in addition, many others about whom we know nothing today. There were vastly different religious viewpoints—the scale runs all the way from Johan Nordal Brun's rich and full-toned Lutheran preaching through a dry orthodoxy and various kinds of neology, to a pure rationalism. The spirit of Enlightenment was still on the upsurge at the end of the century. It reached its high-water mark in the generation that is called the generation of 1814. These men were in the prime of life when Norway gained her independence.

Of Norway's five bishops in 1814, four were rationalists. The fifth was a decided opponent of rationalism. Bergen's Bishop Johan Nordal Brun, the only exception, was a powerful personality, famous as a patriotic poet in the grandiloquent style of the time ("To Norway, homeland of giants, we drink this toast . . ."), and also as a preacher and hymn-writer.

Yet perhaps the most interesting figure among the bishops is Peter Olivarius Bugge, a remarkably complex personality, in whose impetuous temperament the conflicting spiritual currents of the age met. He grew up in a Norwegian parsonage under Moravian influences. As a boy, he had even been taken along on a trip to Herrnhut by an uncle. He began his study in Copenhagen in 1782, where he was ushered into the critical theology of the Enlightenment by his professors, Hornemann and Moldenhawer. At the same time, he was attracted to the theater, like so many other young men of literary ambition. His theology was rationalistic, yet he wrote pietistic poetry. This duplicity came to light in a sensational manner when he in 1795 published the second edition of his *Meditations on the Gospel Texts for the Church Year* (which was marked by substantial pre-rationalistic faith in the Bible, Christocentric piety, and which dwelt emotionally upon Christ's blood atonement), and then took his doctorate at Göttingen in 1796 with a thesis that contained unadulterated rationalism and rejected both original sin and the devil. These two books were reviewed together by an impertinent theological student under the title *A Two-Faced Theologian,* an expression which nearly killed poor Bugge.

After this experience, Bugge chose rationalism for a time. He applied for a call in Denmark in order to escape from his Herrnhutish surroundings in Norway and from his homeland, where he had even been quoted as an authority by the pietistic Haugeans. As a parish pastor in Fredericia from 1799, he wrote a series of rationalistic

works. In 1804, he was appointed Bishop of
Trondheim, a post he had not even sought, by
a church board which saw in him an apostle for
the true enlightenment. During his thirty-eight
years as bishop, a great change came over him.
Very soon the feeling of religious impoverishment
welled up within him again. He interpreted Europe's sufferings in the Napoleonic Era as God's
judgment upon that sinful generation. He grew
disgusted with "the frivolous habits of Copenhagen" and with rationalism. His extremely am-
biguous political position, however, made him
unpopular. In 1814, he was anti-Swedish, and
took a stand for national independence, but when
he crowned Carl Johan King of Norway in 1818,
he used the occasion to deliver a stinging indictment against his countrymen for their arrogance
and national pride. He then proceeded to give
Carl Johan all credit for Norway's freedom before
a packed house of Norwegian and Swedish digni-
taries. That evening, stones were thrown at the
windows of his home. Some of the stones were
wrapped in paper on which were written inscrip-
tions like "Thank you for your speech today,
Bishop" and "Double-tongued Orator!" The theologian with two faces had now been branded as
the orator with two tongues.

The result of all this was that Bugge withdrew

from the world of high society and learning and found his way back to his childhood Christianity and his old milieu, Herrnhutism. He founded a Moravian Society, held Bible studies for the common people, published Norway's first missionary journal, and fought all rationalistic tendencies among the pastors in his diocese.

Bishop Bugge has left us a visitation record spiced with descriptions of the pastors and congregations in his diocese during his long tenure of office. Here we can trace the change which took place among the clergy and the teachers during the first half of the century more clearly than in any other source. He always expressed his judgments in sharp words, and we must bear in mind when using this source that he himself altered his position drastically during his tenure of office.

On his first visitation trips, Bugge comments disparagingly on the old time orthodoxy in preaching and catechization he met in many parishes. More often, however, he met rationalistic preaching. When the pastors preached well and the teachers catechized efficiently in this spirit, he is satisfied. Later, however, and especially after 1818, his condemnation of this type of preaching becomes very severe. "He is ignorant of the basic truths of the Gospel," he writes about one pastor in 1824, and the next year, in another parish, "I heard nothing of Christianity." "Un-Biblical and downright pitiful," "Not pure Christianity," "Bungling naturalism and Socinianism," "Neology," are common evaluations. From this record, it is apparent that rationalistic teaching was rather widespread until the beginning of the 1830's, when a change occurred.

As early as 1819 and following we hear of a teaching of another type. We read constantly of pastors who preach "Christian and Biblical" or "rather Biblical" or "Evangelical" sermons. The change is sometimes discernible among older men who had studied at Copenhagen and who, influenced by the spirit of the times, developed along a more positive Christian line, a development in evidence among many of Bugge's contemporaries also outside his diocese. More often, however, the change occurs where there is a change in personnel. About 1820, a new generation of pastors began to filter into these parishes. In 1820, Bugge heard a sermon in one parish which was "not at all Christian," while this pastor's successor, whom Bugge visited in 1829, preached a "good, Christian" sermon. In another parish, the pastor in 1821 preached a "mediocre, even un-Biblical" sermon, while his successor, four years later, delivered one that was "Biblical in every way."

The line dividing these two generations was so

sharply defined in Norway because of the founding, in 1811, of Norway's own university. From
the time lectures began there in 1813, Norwegian
theological students came under an influence
quite different from that which their older contemporaries had experienced at Copenhagen. The
Theological Faculty at the Norwegian University
consisted of just two men, S. B. Hersleb and St.
J. Stenersen who, until they died in 1836 and
1835 respectively, carried the burden of theological instruction, including elementary Hebrew
and pastoral theology, practically alone. The
Faculty continued to bear their stamp through
their less important successors until the end of the
1840's, when two new young lecturers were appointed. These were to lend a new hue to the
faculty.

Hersleb and Stenersen had both studied at
Copenhagen during the golden age of Enlightenment theology, but they had struck up a friendship with Grundtvig and were, at the time of their
appointment, on the road back to a Biblical, orthodox Christianity and a Lutheran confessionalism. Grundtvig hailed their appointments with
great joy, and wrote that they "now fill the offices
which I for my part consider to be without exaggeration the most important in the world, for
Norway's university is for me the place from

which true Christian theology shall again issue forth into the world."

The two Norwegian professors continued to cultivate their connection with Grundtvig. Stenersen became Grundtvig's defender in Norway, and turned rather aggressively against the unbelief and rationalism of the age. This friendship, however, cooled with the years, and when Grundtvig wrote *The Church's Reply*, in 1825, his two Norwegian friends could no longer follow him. Hersleb and Stenersen trod more and more the path of confessional Lutheranism, and Stenersen wrote a polemic in Norway's first theological journal against Grundtvig's "churchly view." When both Hersleb and Stenersen had passed away, Grundtvig and his Norwegian disciple Wexels agreed (in 1838) that there was "something good and timely in the calling away of these most honorable and beloved men," never suspecting what dark days lay ahead for the "churchly view."

Hersleb and Stenersen had also retained much more of the Enlightenment's theology and historical view of the Bible than Grundtvig in his staunchly Biblical period. In his Bible history for high schools, Hersleb called the creation story an "ancient myth about the creation of the world," while Stenersen allotted nearly half of a textbook in religion for college classes to natural theology.

During the time these men lectured, there arose a generation of theologians who were Biblicists and mildly orthodox Lutherans. These pastors viewed the Haugeaners somewhat sympathetically, although there was indeed a gulf between them and the farmers, who belonged to a different class in a sharply stratified society. They had been taught by their professors that preaching was a matter for the official clergy; they disliked conventicles. The most beautiful expression of the Hersleb-Stenersen pastors' Christianity and message is to be found in M. B. Landstad's hymns and his hymn book of 1869.

When Hersleb died in 1836, the leading Norwegian Grundtvigian W. A. Wexels wrote that Hersleb's eyes had been "dimmed by academic prejudice," so astigmatic that he had been unable to see clearly "the work of the spirit of truth," and therefore he had taken up a position outside "the Church's battle" of that day. "But God has now kindled the light of His Church outside the schools so clearly that even though the schools because of unbelief and false teaching should become a temple of darkness, still the light of the Church is among us." In other words, he was consoled that Norway now had Grundtvigian pastors.

The most distinguished of these pastors was Wexels himself. Born in Copenhagen in 1797, he had attended school there, but when his father moved back to his fatherland in 1814, he enrolled at the university in Christiania. Through Stenersen's lectures, he learned "the very great difference between moral reform and regeneration." He became assistant pastor in Our Savior's Church in Christiania in 1819, pastor in the same church in 1846, remaining in this position until his death in 1866. Thus he was pastor in the same congregation for 47 years and was, in this comparatively unpretentious position, Norway's most influential clergyman in the 1830's, 40's, and 50's. He successfully resisted all attempts to promote him to dean or bishop.

Wexels won recognition with a collection of sermons of a Biblical and churchly Lutheran type in 1822 (the author was then 25 years of age) and with a *Devotional Book for the Parishioner* in 1826. The latter came to be dearly loved by the people of the church and went through many printings. In 1828 he entered the arena as defender of the faith in a controversy which was the exact counterpart to the struggle between Grundtvig and Clausen in Denmark in 1825. In 1828 Niels Treschow, who was the first professor of philosophy at the new Norwegian university and later head of the Ministry for Church Affairs for a number of years, published a book titled *The Spirit of Christianity, or Evangelical Teaching,* in which he displayed a moderate rationalistic theology. The Church's teaching was for Treschow "metaphysical sophistry converted into articles of faith," and he rejected the divinity of Christ and the existence of a personal devil. Wexels countered with a book titled *Thoughts Occasioned by Mr. Treschow's Book Regarding the Truths of Christianity.* The subtitle of the book contained the characteristic word "reply" which occurred in Grundtvig's famous book title in 1825. However, Wexels is more temperate than the author he had chosen as his model, and his arguments stem mainly from the Bible, but he also speaks of "the living confession of the Christian Church throughout all ages" and places himself squarely on Grundtvigian ground. Several other Norwegian Grundtvigians took part in the literary feud which followed. Book titles like *The Voice of Christ's Church Echoes from the Mountains* and *A Serious Word and a Warning Cry From a Son of Old Norway to His Mother and Her Children* are indicative—the first might well have been formulated by Grundtvig himself.

Beginning in the late 1820's, Norway had some Grundtvigian pastors, and small Grundtvigian circles sprang up around them. There was, however, no Grundtvigian parish life, except in one instance, and that one dates from no earlier than the 1850's. Yet there was considerable sympathy for Grundtvigianism in ecclesiastical circles, and in the late 40's most of the elementary school teachers' colleges bore the Grundtvigian stamp.

Grundtvig himself visited Norway for the first and only time in 1851 and was hailed by the students and his co-laborers. At that point, the outlook for a large-scale Grundtvigian movement in Norway was very promising. The periodical *Dansk Kirketidende* made a very optimistic appraisal of the situation and wrote in 1852 that there were many who professed the "churchly view" in Norway. "Yes, it really almost appears that its adherents in Norway already are and still more will become an *Ecclesia Triumphans:* Quite different, therefore, from here in Denmark."

The leading Grundtvigian in Norway analyzes the situation differently. In a letter to his Danish friend Ludvig Helveg in 1847, Wexels wrote: "The clouds are gathering more and more on the horizon *against* the 'churchly view.' It now has a zealous adversary in the Theological Faculty . . . . That *faith* in *the Church* which, after all, is the basis for the churchly view, is for most people an alien thing, indeed a Roman Catholic monster."

A storm had in fact arisen against Wexels and his ecclesiastical ideals among the awakened lay-people. Until the beginning of the 1840's, Wexels had been an authority in the church, beloved and admired by the lay-people for his fight against rationalism and for his popular *Bible History* and his *Devotional Book for the Parishioner*. His popularity, however, came to an abrupt end when a revised *Explanation to Luther's Catechism* was authorized by royal decree in 1843 and ordered introduced into the elementary schools and confirmation instruction. Wexels had been a member of the royal commission which prepared it. The book was a revised edition of Pontoppidan's *Explanation,* which dated from the time of Pietism. However, lay-people who knew their Pontoppidan noticed immediately that "a spirit quite different from that of Pontoppidan flowed through the book," as the first polemic pamphlet from the lay camp put it. Wexels had omitted Pontoppidan's universal condemnation of "novels, dancing and the theater" as *per se* sinful; he had erased the line between the pious and the children of this world and had declared that the Law drives *us* to repentance; he had stated that all baptized were members of the Church; he had called the verbal witness God's Word. But the worst of all was his teaching that Christ preached the Gospel in the kingdom of the dead for "the spirits that were in prison." Such a doctrine held out the possibility of repentance after death, it was said by his opponents, and therefore contradicted the insistence upon the necessity of repentance here and now in this life.

The book called forth several polemical pamphlets from laymen. One self-taught man in Fredrikshald, Olaus Nielsen, edited for ten years his own periodical *Kirkelig Tidende* (circulation two thousand, very high for that time) in which the principal theme was Wexels' *Explanation* and its author, who was portrayed as the beast in the Book of Revelation and as a papist. From all over the country awakened laymen sent resolutions of protest against the revised *Explanation* to the Storting. There were dramatic encounters between awakened farmers and their pastors, one during a visitation of the parish by the Bishop. When the Bishop declared that Wexels would shine brighter in heaven than anybody else he knew, a farmer replied that nobody would be darker in hell. The protests addressed to the Storting were not numerous, the signatures comparatively few, but they were effective. The Government changed its resolution of 1843; in 1852 a royal decree authorized the use also of the old *Explanation*.

The Government capitulated on this point because it feared a free church movement and because it feared a revolution. In 1845, Norway had passed a very liberal (for that time) Dissenter Law; the dissatisfied might easily have broken away from the church and organized free congregations. Church leaders feared a mass withdrawal. Moreover, the memory of France's February Revolution was still fresh in their minds, and in Norway the first organized labor movement had been suppressed in 1851.

The *Explanation* decision of 1852 represented a victory for the pietistic orthodoxy of the laymen over Grundtvigian ecclesiasticism, a victory for the lay movement over the clergy, and a victory for the farmers over the official class. During the struggle, Olaus Nielsen wrote: "Think what power the Lord entrusted to the people through Hans Nielsen Hauge's work! Should we not now use this mighty gift?"

Meanwhile, in that very hour, the awakened laymen had found a powerful ally in the Theological Faculty, and this constellation could to a large extent bear out Wexels' pessimistic words that the clouds were gathering on the horizon against the churchly and culturally interested type of Christianity he represented.

Chapter Two

The Johnsonian Revival
The Inner Mission Movement
The Struggle Over Grundtvigianism

In the 1850's and 60's, an awakening swept over all of Norway; it is called the Johnsonian Revival, after Professor Gisle Johnson, who did not set it in motion but was himself gripped by it at an early stage and thereafter became its leading personality. In its broad effect upon Norwegian society and its significance for the ecclesiastical development in Norway, this awakening undoubtedly surpasses the Hauge movement.

The awakening's explosion was not touched off by any one personality. The Norwegian Missionary Society was established in 1842, and the many missions meetings which followed in various parts of the country had an awakening effect. There were also several local awakening efforts. Pastor Lyder Brun, grandson of Bishop Johan Nordal Brun, passed through a religious crisis in the mid-40's, and then emerged as a revival preacher, pro-

35

voking spiritual movements in various places, notably among the patrician class in Bergen. To Skien in 1848 came Gustav Adolph Lammers as parish pastor, a powerful preacher of repentance and a zealous shepherd of souls. He preached eloquently and authoritatively in a pietistic spirit, and people even from outside his parish flocked to hear him. He went from house to house ministering to people's spiritual needs, and sought to separate the faithful from the worldly by a system of church discipline revolving around Holy Communion.

It was Johnson's advent as a preacher that brought the awakening to the capital city. It is possible that he had been influenced by Lammers; Johnson himself says that Lammers was dear to his heart as only few persons were.

When Candidate of Theology Gisle Johnson was appointed lecturer in theology at the University in 1849, he was a man of twenty-seven years who already commanded respect as a great theological light in Norway. In 1851, at the invitation of one of the city's pastors, he began to hold Bible studies in Christiania. Johnson himself was not an ordained clergyman, and he stated in his old age that it had often been a comfort to him that one of the Church's ordained servants had invited him to hold public Bible studies.

Johnson's devotional meetings were held in the most widely different places in the city, eventually settling in the cathedral. People streamed to the meetings; Johnson often spoke for two full hours or longer.

It is strange that this man should have been a popular preacher of repentance. He came from a family of state officials and was far removed from the masses. He was quiet and shy, and his religious growth had been harmonious. But he possessed a remarkable ability as a preacher. The whole congregation would tremble when Johnson quietly and in a thin voice quoted the prophet's words: "There is no peace for the ungodly, saith my God."

A cholera epidemic in 1853 accentuated the serious mood in the capital. The revival placed its mark on Christiania to such an extent, says Johnson's disciple Bishop Heuch, that one "was reminded of Palm Sunday, when everyone wanted to be a disciple and cry 'Hosanna,' while the opponents had to be content to stand in the corners and grumble."

Johnson's influence as a preacher also spread outside of Christiania, through his vacation trips and his participation in pastoral conferences. He even travelled as a revival strategist to those places in Norway where there was spiritual unrest. In

1856, for example, he went all the way to Tromsø, where the Lammers movement and Anabaptist propaganda had made the situation unsettled. Several times on these journeys he held devotional gatherings together with Haugean lay-preachers, a fact which awakened great interest among the lay people.

The Johnsonian revival ushered in a new relationship between the state church officials and the awakened groups throughout Norway. It also bridged the gap between social classes which had formerly given rise to the assumption that there was one religion for the cultured people and another for the masses.

Johnson's preaching activity lasted for ten years; it came to an end early in the 1860's. He was then a burned-out man. He ceased preaching; his lectures became progressively dryer, containing little that was stimulating. By that time, however, the revival had spread over the entire country, and it continued through Johnson's disciples. One of these, who had been seized by the revival in the 50's, has described how it spread through many channels: "The theological students wrote letters to their parents, their brothers and sisters, their fiancées, their friends and acquaintances. They came home on vacation, held devotions, prayed, and exhorted. Young ladies brought the movement with them when they visited their girl friends. The vacation centers were often centers for the movement during the summer months, whence it was extended back into 'the thousand homes.' "

During the 1850's and 60's, the revival changed the lives of huge segments of the Norwegian people. The change in parsonage life is tangible evidence of this. A theological student who visited Skjeberg parsonage in 1854 and again in 1856 describes his second visit: "Skjeberg parsonage had previously been noted for its hospitality and great conviviality. Nearly every Sunday, when there was a service in the church, there were a great many out-of-town guests; on Sunday afternoons, the men frequently sat at the card table. . . . All this is changed now. The custom of inviting guests was discontinued, the card tables disappeared, and with a view to the servants also having a day of rest, the assistant pastor and his family have this last year ceased to visit the pastor on Sunday as before. Instead, these things have been supplanted by the reading of God's Word, singing, prayer, and conversations on spiritual matters."

The poet Vinje, who disliked the Johnsonian revival, has described in his *Travel Memoirs* from the summer of 1860 how an entire city

changed character under the influence of the revival. When he visited Christiansund, he had been
impressed by the culture and wealth of initiative
among the rich merchants there. They "could
speak about art and literary matters like learned
men of the better sort." But now these enlightened
people were tied down by an ignorant crowd "who
oppressed the city with their faith." He says that
a young pastor had brought this religious epidemic to the city. The intelligentsia dared not
speak out because such things must have their day.
"It never does a particle of good to speak against
these things while they are in progress; it only
makes people consider you a godless person."

That the revival spread so widely throughout
the country and into all classes of society was precisely due to the fact that it was borne by the pastors. Those who were most strongly influenced
by Gisle Johnson were his students. Most of the
young men who studied theology during the first
three or four decades of his forty-five year teaching
ministry went out as Johnsonians. Thanks to this
zealous generation of pastors, Norwegian church
life became thoroughly colored by Johnsonian
orthodoxy and pietism.

The effects of the revival showed up in Norwegian intellectual life as a whole. Lutheran orthodoxy was the predominant trend in Norway

until the late 70's. At any rate, Johnsonian theology determined the limits of what scholars and
authors could say publicly.

The philosopher Waldemar Dons, who himself
suffered certain unpleasant consequences because
he had in 1880 polemicized against Johnson in his
lectures, later wrote in retrospect concerning the
revival (not without bitterness and with some
exaggeration) that Johnson at the height of his
power "ruled over all the pulpits and meeting-
house lecterns and through them everything that
was called official or private Christianity—the
whole country, the entire populace, all the way
from the lecture halls of the University and the
departmental offices to the poorest tenant shack;
yes, it is literally true—all the way from the ball-
room to the most wretched tavern in the slums of
Christiania."

For most of his students, Johnson's lectures during the 1850's and 60's were thoroughly fascinating. He drove home the points of Lutheran orthodoxy with a heartfelt religious sincerity, a pene-
trating logic, and a gift for psychological analysis
of the soul's religious life which overwhelmed
them. His theology was a Lutheran orthodoxy in
completely modern dress. Johnson had been overwhelmed by the ideas of Kierkegaard in the late
40's and early 50's; the melancholy Dane now un-

derwent the thing he detested most of all, incorporation into a system, the basic framework of which Johnson took from the contemporary Erlangen school (Hofmann, Frank, Thomasius). This system was appropriated by all of Johnson's pupils and reproduced in examination even in his very words.

It was prefaced by a theological discipline which he called "pistics," the doctrine of the genesis of faith, in which Johnson formulated his own version of Kierkegaard's doctrine of the stages of human life. Natural man's existence is characterized by egoism, disharmony, suffering and fear. This points forward to a higher stage which can only be reached by a leap: man's existence under the law. But the despair which follows upon legalism points in turn toward the highest stage, the Christian faith, which is "a particular form of man's personal existence." Expanding the content of faith into a dogmatic, Johnson allows this unfolding to take the form of an analysis of the Christian's "consciousness of salvation" and of the ideas which are contained in, or presupposed in, this consciousness of salvation. At all points, he comes up with exactly the same conclusions as are contained in the Lutheran confessional writings. He then demonstrates that these, in turn, are in full agreement with the Bible.

Johnson followed one method in all his polemic. He first confronted the opponents with the Lutheran Confessions and the statements of Luther. "Lutheran" and "un-Lutheran" became the decisive theological arguments. An opponent was doomed when he had been branded as un-Lutheran, whereupon there usually followed a demonstration that in the point at issue the Lutheran standpoint was also that of the Bible.

This Johnsonian form of confessionalism came to place its mark upon several generations of pastors; we can see its effects in Norwegian church life today, where Lutheran confessionalism remains on the throne. Everything started by Johnson and his disciples has the word "Lutheran" in its name: *Theologisk Tidsskrift for den evangelisk-lutherske Kirke i Norge, Luthersk Kirketidende, Luthersk Ugeskrift, Ny luthersk Kirketidende, Lutherstiftelsen, Det norske lutherske Indremissionsselskab.*

The ethos of the revival was a rather somber pietism. Theoretically, Johnson and the Johnsonian theologians asserted Christian liberty and warned against pietistic legalism, but in practice abstinence from the adiaphora was made a necessity. Johnson himself smoked a pipe and allowed young people to dance *Francaise* in his house, and several writers of memoirs are eager to relate that

they recall definite occasions when he laughed
heartily (the best proof that he did not laugh
often). The outside world, however, knew him
only as a serious man who, with tearful voice,
proclaimed the seriousness of the final accounting.

Beginning in the 1850's, the Johnsonian pastors,
with their zealous orthodoxy and pietism began
to replace the old Hersleb-Stenersen men. The relationship between these generations of clergymen
was often felt to be one of direct opposition. In
several of Alexander Kielland's novels the two
types confront one another—the old parish pastor,
a state church official with a good conscience, non-
pietistic and culturally interested, an aristocrat
who keeps himself aloof from the awakened, and
the young Johnsonian assistant pastor, pietistic,
sociable toward the awakened, a zealous revival
preacher and state-church official with a bad conscience.

However, because the older generation was not
belligerent, the contrast between these two generations did not emerge as sharply as it might. Some
of the older men were themselves seized by the
new currents; the others refused to do battle.
Christopher Bruun, who had sat at Johnson's feet
without becoming a Johnsonian—he preferred, to
use his own words, to struggle with Kierkegaard's
paradoxes rather than to swallow the Johnsonian

porridge—reports that the older pastors felt there was something unhealthy about the new age, but "they were not fighters," he adds. "Trapped between the shields of farmer piety on one side and those of professor superiority on the other, they bowed their graying heads and surrendered."

The Johnsonian pastors considered themselves spokesmen for Christianity in dead state-church congregations. Theirs was a missionary task, and the congregations were the mission fields. They spoke to the individual; all sought to be revival preachers. Mass Christianity, Christian institutions and forms, and the Christian traditions of a nation counted for little in their estimation. On the subject of the sacraments they said little more than that a person must not rely upon his infant baptism and that he must beware of partaking unworthily of the Lord's Supper, thus eating and drinking damnation upon himself.

The result of this preaching was that people stayed away from the Lord's Table. While churchgoing and attendance at Christian meetings reached an all-time high, communicant participation dropped off enormously. The old type Communion attended by practically all in the spring and fall, a continuation of the mass Communion at Easter in Catholic times, was on the wane when the revival set in, and the Johnsonian pastors suc-

ceeded in eradicating it completely. The Johnsonian zealot Karl Roll left the parish ministry,
spent several years as prison chaplain and later as
superintendent of the missionary school, because
his ecclesiastical superiors would not allow him
to turn away communicants. Not until 1878 would
his conscience again permit him to take a call to
the parish, and then only because there were so
few who went to Communion. The Johnsonians
made Communion a service for the few who had
their accounts with God in order; when not even
these ventured to attend, they began to preach
complainingly about the lack of understanding
for the Holy Communion among the believers, a
lack which they themselves had elicited.

The Johnsonians' neglect of baptism ought to
have prepared an excellent seed-bed for the Baptist propaganda which also began in Norway during the 50's. That this propaganda led, however, to
prodigiously small results was due to the strongly
confessional spirit among the church people. For
hundreds of years the people had been brought up
in Lutheranism, and both the Hauge awakening
and the Johnsonian revival underlined the confessional element. It was useless to present a teaching that was not Lutheran.

Two pastoral duties, in particular, caused pangs
of conscience among the Johnsonian clergy: con-

firmation and confession. In general, they favored abolishing compulsory confirmation and compulsory church marriage, in order that they might weed out unrepentant confirmands and maintain church discipline in the consecration of marriages. Some few also opposed the state-church and deserted it. One such instance caused a sensation in 1856. Pastor Lammers in Skien first applied for his dismissal because he could not submit to the church's practice regarding confession and declare the forgiveness of sins to impenitent people. Some weeks later, influenced by Kierkegaard's *The Moment,* he walked out of the state-church and established a free congregation. Lammers' congregation soon became Baptist. He himself returned to the state-church some years later. Two similar cases of official resignation in the mid-70's led to the establishment of the Lutheran Free Church, which characteristically enough became the largest of the free church denominations and remained so until the Second World War.

Several of the theologians who were young in the 50's nursed serious misgivings about becoming pastors. In 1855 Candidate of Theology Nils Hertzberg introduced a discussion in the Students' Association with the question: "Is it defensible to become a pastor in the state church?" and replied in the negative, "since I reasoned from Kierke-

gaardian premises." Some of his contemporaries
served in educational positions and waited years
before seeking calls to the parish. A few never became pastors, among them Nils Hertzberg himself,
though he did become Minister of Church Affairs,
which, reasoning from Kierkegaardian premises,
was not much better than becoming a pastor.

Many of the Johnsonians worked zealously to
loosen the more stringent state-church ties. They
championed the right of state officials to leave the
state-church, the right of civil marriage, and other
reforms, and favored the introduction of parish
councils. Yet most of them advocated stringent
voting requirements so as to ensure that the
awakened, not the unrepentant masses, would
govern the church. Efforts for more religious freedom bore fruit in a series of legal changes, especially after the Liberal Party rode to power with
the introduction of the parliamentary system in
1884. On the other hand, ecclesiastical self-gov-
ernment and parish councils were temporarily
shelved, because of strong clergy opposition, lack
of lay interest, and the Storting's unwillingness to
surrender control of the church to the pietistic
pastors and laymen.

From the very beginning, cordial relations
existed between the awakened lay people and the

Johnsonian pastors. Under clerical leadership, the lay movement passed over into its organized stage in the 50's. Lammers established the first inner missions association at Skien in 1853. This example was soon (1855) followed in the capital, and later in many places throughout the country. The first meeting-place to bear the name "Prayer-House" was also built at Skien, in 1850. During the decades that followed, the vast majority of congregations built their own prayer-houses for Bible classes and devotional meetings, activities which, according to then existing legislation, could not take place in the churches. We thus pass over into the period of the prayer-houses and the Christian meetings. The pastor's work changed character. Prayer-house activities came to comprise a large part of it. When Bishop Niels Jacob Laache died in 1892, *Luthersk Kirketidende* wrote that he had been a bishop after the layman's own heart, and continued by saying, "I recall very few of the larger bazaars at which the Bishop did not put in one or two appearances." Compared to the men of 1814, this was indeed a new type of bishop!

The awakened lay-people soon found their natural place in the Inner Mission associations. In many places they elected the pastor to the chairmanship. But there were not always harmonious relationships between pastor and association. In

Christiania the clergy, led by the Dean and Pastor
Wexels, gave the local association for home missions a somewhat conditional blessing upon its
inauguration. Their letter stated, among other
things, they did not consider it proper for them to
become members of the association, and pointed
at sectarianism and pharisaism as imminent dangers for the association. In Bergen, the inner mission association was established without the participation of the clergy, and when the pastors of
Bergen requested that the statutes should be
changed so that the clergy would always have a
certain number of representatives on the board,
they met with determined opposition. The laymen
refused to concede the pastors any favored position in the association, but expressed their desire
to cooperate with them in inner missions work.

The tense relation between the clergy and the
inner missions people was brought more sharply
into focus in 1868 when an organization for inner
missions work on a nation-wide scale, modelled
after the Swedish *Fosterlandsstiftelse,* was established under the name *Den Norske Lutherstiftelse.*
Originally, *Lutherstiftelsen* was a working committee in the capital, but local associations could
unite with the committee and thereby receive
certain privileges. Thus, a nation-wide society for
inner missions was built up. Even before the

organization of *Lutherstiftelsen,* fourteen of Christiania's seventeen pastors, headed by the bishop and the dean, issued a statement in which they dissociated themselves from the new organization and stated that its administration would come to be "a second church administration" and that it would in reality one day "examine and appoint to the Service of the Word, a Service which can never be called private."

Gisle Johnson was one of the founders of *Lutherstiftelsen* and was its chairman, except for brief periods, until 1891. During all this time, *Lutherstiftelsen* was based upon what Johnson called "the emergency principle." "The great spiritual need" in the church was of an extraordinary nature and demanded extraordinary measures, it was stated in the invitation to the founding. The new institution was to work primarily through the printed word. Its publications were to be circulated by colporteurs or "Bible messengers" who would also converse with individuals and hold family devotions, whenever the master of the house desired. As to how far the Bible messengers could go in preaching, it was said at the founding that "there exists a need which entitles also such people as are not regularly called by the church to come forward and publicly proclaim God's Word," and it was stated that "The

Lord has richly blessed such lay-preaching." At the same time, however, *Lutherstiftelsen* would not authorize anyone to preach and thus give him a right which each man already has when he is driven by the Spirit to bear witness.

The background for these declarations lay in the fact that lay-preaching was not exactly easy to reconcile with Article 14 of the Augsburg Confession, which states that no one may preach publicly unless he be "rightly called," *rite vocatus*. After 1842, there was no ban on lay-preaching in the civil law. But now the question arose with renewed vigor whether or not it really was ecclesiastically legitimate. The question was particularly annoying because Johnson and his disciples always appealed so strongly to the Lutheran confessional writings. Johnson attempted to skirt the difficulty by constantly referring to the need which made churchly irregularities legitimate and by allowing *Lutherstiftelsen's* claim that, while it could not take responsibility for lay-preaching, it would not forbid it but would rather encourage it. In practice, therefore, the Bible messengers very soon made their appearance as preachers, and to an ever-increasing extent.

The Johnsonian "emergency principle" was violently assailed from two quarters in the lively debate over lay-preaching which took place in the

1860's and 70's. There was a high-church wing
whose high-churchmanship consisted in a solid
Lutheran doctrine accompanied by a high conception of the ministerial office, a conservative contentment with the state church, and a rejection of
reforms aiming at greater religious freedom or
development of a democratic church order. To
this group belonged the majority of the clergy
and all who had right-wing political leanings in
the 60's and 70's. This element constantly emphasized Article 14 of the Augustana, pointing out
that lay-preaching without a license from the
Church authorities was contrary to the Lutheran
Confession, and that the circumstances were especially aggravated when this activity was carried
on by an organization which in reality authorized
and sent out preachers. Leading high-church men
like Pastor (later Bishop) J. C. Heuch did not,
however, seek to forbid lay preaching, but instead
sought to channel it into churchly forms. If lay-
preachers were examined by a bishop and commissioned by him, the institution would be accept-
able from the Church's point of view. This proposal met with strong criticism from lay circles,
where it was thought that such a plan would de-
prive the lay movement of its freedom and place
it under the Establishment. A bill for the founding of a diaconate with churchly consecration of

lay-preachers was voted down by the Storting by a large majority in 1888.

The left wing of the church was no less dissatisfied with Johnson's emergency principle. This discontent was expressed in open criticism, but particularly also in the fact that many local inner mission associations refused to ally themselves with *Lutherstiftelsen*.

In the mid-70's, the situation in church politics became acute. Gisle Johnson resigned the editorship of *Luthersk Kirketidende* in 1875, and was succeeded by Professor F. W. Bugge and Pastor J. C. Heuch, two high-church theologians who immediately began to polemicize against lay activity in this, *Lutherstiftelsen's* own periodical. After one year they were summarily dismissed as editors and replaced by two low-church pastors. In 1877 Bugge and Heuch founded their own periodical, the high-churchly *Luthersk Ugeskrift*. About the same time, a new church periodical appeared in Bergen under the title *Ny Luthersk Kirketidende,* organ for the extreme low-church wing which repudiated the emergency principle and stood for full religious freedom and a democratic church constitution based upon the broadest possible suffrage.

Parallel with the literary dispute over lay-preaching in the three weekly church periodicals a struggle was raging in the congregations. The clergy went through the same experience as had the thirteenth century parish clergy when the mendicant monks began to infiltrate their congregations. Preachers who, to be sure, belonged to the same church, but who had not had the same training, whose religious ideals were somewhat different, and who were mostly common folk, invaded their domain, sent out by a central agency. Many pastors received the lay-preachers well—it was an easy step for all the Johnsonians who had followed their teacher also in church politics. The high-churchly pastors, on the other hand, were very cool toward the lay-preachers who came into their congregations.

In the early 80's the debate of Article 14 of the Augustana subsided completely. J. C. Heuch and with him all the other high-church men now discovered far more threatening dangers which demanded the marshalling of all forces in opposition: Political liberalism and modern unbelief. They could no longer afford to continue the hopeless fight against lay-preaching. They had to mobilize also the left wing of the church for the far greater battle at hand. The result was expressed in a rather cynical manner by a layman at the diocesan meeting in Bergen in 1877 when he said that Article 14 ought now to be buried. It was

indeed buried so deep that it has hardly been
heard of since, least of all from the elements who
in succeeding generations have laid special claim
to confessional fidelity.

With the High Court of Justice decision against
Prime Minister Selmer in 1884, the principle
triumphed that a government cannot act contrary
to a majority vote in the Storting. The guarantee
for the church's secure existence which Heuch and
his partisans had found in the (until then) always conservative government, which could defend the church against a Liberal majority in the
Storting, was gone. Norway got a parliamentary
liberal government, led by Johan Sverdrup, with
the radically low-church Pastor Jakob Sverdrup
as a member and soon to be Minister for Church
Affairs. In this situation the high-church pastors
became adherents of the idea of a church constitution, although with a stipulation for confessional loyalty as a condition for the church fran-
chise. They sought allies, and gave up their
opposition to lay-preaching.

The low-church wing scored victory after victory, while the high-church party grimly faced disintegration. In 1884 the Storting had passed by a
large majority a law which gave pastors permission to use the churches for meetings other than
Sunday services and to allow laymen to speak

in the churches. The law was refused royal sanction on the grounds that, according to Norwegian
constitutional law, legislation regarding religious
rites lay outside the jurisdiction of the Storting.
The King prescribes all public church services,
says the Constitution. Jakob Sverdrup did not
learn this constitutional nicety in vain. When he
became Minister for Church Affairs, he saw to it
that two royal decrees were promulgated: One
which gave laymen permission to speak in the
churches (1888), and one which opened the
churches for "churchly meetings relating to either
foreign or home missions" (1889).

The lay movement was now accepted both by
popular church opinion and in the law-books.
The next stage was a further consolidation of
the movement. The majority of inner missions
supporters had hitherto remained outside of
Lutherstiftelsen because of the emergency principle. Several times around 1890 the plea for a
union of all inner mission associations had been
heard, but it could be accomplished only by aban-
doning the emergency principle. *Lutherstiftelsen* accordingly agreed at its general meeting
in 1891 to drop the emergency principle, and
undertook an important reorganization. Its name
was changed to *Det Norske Lutherske Indremissionsselskab*. Gisle Johnson disapproved of aban-

doning the emergency principle and retired as chairman, but remained on the board.

Simultaneously, the high-church wing completely collapsed. When its leader, J. C. Heuch, became bishop in 1889, he became particularly friendly to the laymen. A remarkable metamorphosis which had begun some years earlier was now quickly consummated. The highly aristocratic Heuch, who had demanded examination of lay-preachers by the ecclesiastical authorities, now dealt with lay-preachers on the most friendly terms, constantly took part in prayer-house meetings, and tolerated violations of the ecclesiastical order and strong remarks against the clergy. He worked zealously for a union of all friends of inner mission. The explanation for his transformation lies in the fact that he needed a strong ally in the battle against modern unbelief and especially against liberal theology within the church. To defend the faith he gave up his views on the ministry.

The most important theologian in the high-church ranks, the learned dogmatician Krogh-Tonning, evinced an ever-increasing sympathy with the Roman Church during the 1890's, and eventually went over to that church body in 1900. Heuch's co-editor on *Luthersk Ugeskrift* in the 80's, Pastor M. J. Faerden, trod quite another path. From the early 90's, he developed into a liberal and a zealous popularizer of the results of Biblical criticism. The collapse of the high-church front was complete.

We left the story of Grundtvigianism just at the point when it had become a strong influence in Norwegian church life, but when the clouds were gathering on the horizon for a coming storm. After 1850 the Grundtvigian tide was to reach its peak, but Grundtvigianism was also to meet with violent opposition and after some decades to disintegrate as an ecclesiastical party.

Among the clergy during the 1850's the Grundt-vigians loomed large, under the leadership of "old Wexels," as he was often called; they included such men as Wexels' nephew Fredrik Wexelsen, Carl Wille, H. Steensrud, and C. U. Sundt. The teaching profession also supported the Grundt-vigian movement. In the 50's Norway had a gene-ration of enthusiastic men who stood for popular education, who had a faith in the people and their possibilities coupled with a church-minded and culturally interested Christianity. Ole Vig and Anders Reitan were the leaders.

Yet this religious movement, with its faith in the baptismal covenant, its interest in humanity, and its emphasis on the national church, also met with intense opposition from three directions: from the Theological Faculty and the Johnsonian pastors, from the awakened laymen, and from the church administration in the government.

The difference between the two positions which joined battle in the 50's and 60's was interpreted by contemporaries as a difference of opinion over certain theological questions. It was a struggle between "Scriptural theologians" and adherents of the theory that the Apostles' Creed was a word from the Lord's mouth, preserved in unaltered form through all ages of the Church. When the struggle is so interpreted, it is not the least bit strange that the Grundtvigians drew the shortest straw, for it was not particularly difficult to show that the Grundtvigian theory was the purest fancy.

The conflict, however, did not really concern theological doctrines. There were two views of life which stood in opposition to one another. Wexels described in 1861 the beneficial effects of the "Grundtvigian enlightenment" in this way: It had "fostered a blessed, kindly, cheerful life, rich in praise, with an open eye for all God's works in human life." In 1863, Gisle Johnson wrote in a review of Bishop Martensen's treatise against Grundtvigianism that he disagreed with Martensen when the Bishop said that the debate with the Grundtvigians revolved about a differ-

ence of opinion "within the Christian (realm)."
The Danish Bishop had not caught sight of
Grundtvigianism's "whole basic fallacy and basic
fatality." Its "basic delusion" was its "failure to
view man's sinful depravity in all its depth."

From the very beginning of his career as lecturer at the University, Johnson had declared war
on Grundtvigianism. It was "un-Lutheran" and
therefore "un-churchly." The Grundtvigians "eat
the Church's bread and tear down its walls," he
declared, directing his remarks at Wexels.

The Theological Faculty was wholly on Johnson's side. In its instruction, the Lutheran Scriptural principle and the doctrine of the total depravity of man were emphasized and examination
questions over this material frequently assigned,
particularly when the Faculty suspected that students with Grundtvigian leanings were up for
examination. Deviations from the true doctrine
were recompensed with poor grades.

At Johnson's side stood Professor Carl Paul
Caspari, a unique research scholar. He was a German Jew, brought up in the Jewish faith, but he
had accepted baptism at the age of twenty-four
and studied oriental languages and Old Testament theology. He had already made a name for
himself as an orientalist when Johnson met him
on a study tour in Leipzig in 1846 and persuaded

him to apply for a position at the University of
Christiania. He had declined a call to Königsberg
because the Prussian Church was a union church,
but the Faculty in Christiania attracted him because it was entirely Lutheran. He moved to Norway in 1847 and remained professor in Christiania
until his death in 1892, despite attractive offers
from German universities.

Caspari was soon mobilized into the Norwegian
spiritual struggle. Grundtvigianism's assertions
about the Apostles' Creed offended both the Lutheran and the historian in him. He made it
his task to disprove historically the "churchly
view." From the mid-50's until his death, he
expended the greatest share of his time and
energy in a study of the history of the baptismal
confession and disseminated a series of scholarly
works in Norwegian and German on the history
of symbols. Readers outside Scandinavia could
hardly suspect that these learned and temperate
historical discussions had a polemic aim, but in
Denmark and Norway this aspect of his disser-
tations was clearly perceived. A reviewer in *Dansk
Kirketidende* observed that Caspari was "blind to
the faith of the congregation," while the Norwegian pietists were jubilant because Caspari had
refuted the Grundtvigians.

In the parishes Grundtvigian pastors and teachers frequently met a solid wall of opposition. The bone of contention between pastor and congregation was usually the wording of the Apostles' Creed. The pastor used the historically correct wording ("the holy catholic Church, the communion of saints") while the awakened laymen demanded that he stick to the form in the altar book ("I believe that there exists a holy Christian Church, which is the communion of holy men"). Parish Pastor Gunnerus was fined by the Supreme Court in 1872 for having withstood the demands of his parishioners that he use the altar book version of the confession of faith. He tendered his resignation, and was soon followed by another Grundtvigian who also had found himself in an untenable position with his congregation.*

The Minister of Church Affairs had wanted Gunnerus discharged, and in this and analogous instances, the Ministry was constantly unwilling to untangle the mess by transferring the Grundtvigian pastors. Teachers with similar tendencies were also usually denied transfer. The Ministry's hostile attitude was further revealed when the first Grundtvigian Folk High School was founded in 1864 at Sagatun, near Hamar. As a counter-

---

*TRANSLATOR'S NOTE: This pastor was J. W. C. Dietrichson, founder of the Lutheran congregation at Koshkonong, Wis., who spent six years in America (1844-50). He left the ministry in 1876 for the Norwegian postal service. His return to Norway marked the end of Grundtvigianism among the Norwegians in America.

move, a new teachers' seminary was located at
Hamar and the faculty positions filled with Johnsonian theologians.

Of course, adversity could not crush Grundtvigianism. It could only turn it into a sharply
defined and strongly besieged little faction in the
nation's church life. The movement's ruin was
wrought by an inner crisis.

After Grundtvig's death in 1872, Bjørnstjerne
Bjørnson loomed as the coming leader of both
the Danish and the Norwegian Grundtvigians.
But he straightway made his position in Denmark
impossible by his utterances concerning that country's relations with Germany, and he soon revealed
that he was no religious leader. Bjørnson had
never grasped more than one side of Grundtvigianism, that it was a popular liberal cultural
movement. When he leveled a polemic blast
against dogmatic Christianity at the end of the
70's, the Norwegian Grundtvigians were split, and
their rivals triumphantly pointed at what Grundtvigianism led to. This split in Grundtvigian ranks
was made manifest at the so-called spiritual freedom meeting at Sagatun in 1886. The old-Grundt-
vigian minority, under Fr. Wexelsen and Christopher Bruun, continued their stand on the baptismal covenant with its renunciation of the devil,
and confession of faith, while the more numerous

neo-Grundtvigians interpreted the movement as a liberal cultural movement and made common cause with the free-thinkers. When their leader Viggo Ullmann was upbraided for having broken with the genuine Grundtvigian line, he wrote irritatedly in 1888, "I should like to see 'genuine Grundtvigianism,' like 'genuine Lutheranism' banished from the earth. We need human beings with kind hearts and open minds, not these 'genuine' gentlemen of Luther's house and Grundtvig's stock, theologians of theologians, orthodox men of white or light-gray color."

Grundtvigianism foundered as an ecclesiastical party, but its influence remained in the church. Grundtvig's hymns had found a place in the hymn books, and the Apostles' Creed was in 1887 made an integral part of the liturgy. The historically correct form was prescribed, although the incorrect altar-book form was permitted as well. Also remaining as a heritage for future generations was an understanding of the church as the spiritual home of the entire nation and of the concept of a national church. These were later to be accentuated by the *Landsmaal* movement at the end of the century.

Grundtvigianism was thus transformed from an ecclesiastical party into a stimulus in the life of the church.

Chapter Three

The Crisis of the 1880's
The Conflict Over Liberal Theology

During the 1870's and 80's Norway's spiritual climate altered markedly within a few years. In the intellectual life the school of positivism entered upon the scene, with its belief in cultural progress, its religious skepticism and relativistic view of Christian dogma, its whole structure grounded in modern natural science and Biblical criticism.

This movement was late in arriving in Norway; here as in no other country orthodox Lutheran theology had dominated the scene clear up until the beginning of the 70's. Therefore, when it finally did come, positivism descended upon Norway like a landslide.

There were several in the 70's who anticipated the coming revolt. One of these was Bjørnstjerne Bjørnson. In a series of newspaper articles during the summer of 1876 signed "A Christian," he levelled a blast at the reigning orthodoxy and

66

pietism which he said would stand powerless when "unbelief's well-equipped thought and doubt finally cross the border." When that day comes, "what will happen to the church's preaching? It will have to take what it deserves. But what will happen to Christianity? The answer is indicated in the history of other lands."

The changing spirit of the times during the 70's and 80's has been described and analyzed from year to year in a series of annual surveys on Norwegian church life by a keen observer, Pastor Thv. Klaveness. In 1874 he was of the opinion that "the streams of unbelief which have passed over other countries have really not yet reached into our fjords and valleys." "However, this era seems about to end," he continues. Unbelief has already reared its head, "both in speech and in writing." Frivolous and unchristian foreign novels are being read in our country, too. The Sabbath has begun to lose its character as a holy day, through "excessive Sunday travel by train and steamer." In 1877 he reports that there are "parts of our country and groups within our people which are turning their backs upon the Church and God's Word." Old-time conventional Christianity is on the point of being superseded by "complete indifference" which in turn leads to "wanton unbelief." One meets with rancorous attacks on the church and the clergy. The tally of Communion guests is dropping off alarmingly. "One still dares to maintain," says he in 1878, "that public opinion is surely on the side of the Christian faith." Still, the more positivistic professors Norway gets, the easier it is for the young students to become "the prey of unbelief." And the radical newspapers are at work spreading unbelief among the people. In 1882 Klaveness tells his Swedish readers, "This age's modern unbelief, together with its confederate, political liberalism, is making great strides among our people, and at a speed which no one would have thought possible a few years ago."

There is no doubt that Klaveness was correct. The positivistic trend was making rapid advances in Norwegian learning, public debate, and literature.

Positivism entered the University through the persons of the Sars brothers. Ossian Sars became professor of zoology in 1874 and lectured on the theory of evolution, while Ernst Sars, who became professor of history the same year, gave a fascinating general survey of Norwegian history from a positivistic viewpoint. His appointment had met with opposition. A very churchly and orthodox professor of medicine protested against attaching an adherent of the positivistic school to the University. For the positivists, he said, "history is a development based essentially upon natural presuppositions."

Appointment of the Sars brothers implied an adoption in principle of the idea that the University was not bound to any particular view of life, even though both the Minister for Church Affairs and Ernst Sars glossed over the situation by saying that he was not a positivist, viz., in the sense that he adhered to Comte's philosophy. That the University was not, however, completely indifferent to questions relating to religion came to light when in 1876 Georg Brandes, the foremost spokesman for positivism in Scandinavia, was denied use of the University's halls and was consequently forced to use the Students' Association hall for his lectures on Kierkegaard. On the other hand, a positivistic literary historian and a Darwinistic botanist were appointed to the faculty without incident, in 1877 and 1880 respectively. In 1880, Brandes again visited Christiania, and this time he was allowed to lecture in the University. Positivism's homestead claim on the University campus could no longer be disputed.

Positivism strongly asserted itself in periodicals and newspapers. As early as the late 60's, a literary magazine called *Norden* had voiced belief in evolution and had cautiously criticized Norwegian church life from the standpoint of positivism. From 1865-79 the politician Søren Jaabaek, an enemy of the clergy, edited a remarkable periodical called *Folketidende* in which he disseminated propoganda for his own political and religious opinions for a wide circle of readers. The publication had at one time a circulation of seventeen thousand throughout the country. He constantly hounded the clergy, whom he called swindlers of the people.

Nyt Norsk Tidsskrift made its debut in 1877. During its two-year life span, it was filled with articles about positivism, the theory of evolution, and the proofs of Biblical criticism for the existence of contradictory sources in the Old Testament. Its editors say they do not deny the need of religion, but it must remain within the limits set down by science and must "confine itself to upholding the great mystery of which nothing can be said except that it exists."

When *Nyt Norsk Tidsskrift* failed, its work was continued by *Nyt Tidsskrift,* organ for the positivistic cultural front during the 80's. *Nyt Tidsskrift* kept a watchful eye on Norway's theologians and their literary productions, which were always commented upon without mercy. There were many articles on the theory of evolution, on man's place in nature, on Darwin's view of religion, and on mankind's religious development. Positivism's view of life and its criticism of Christianity also found expression in this review in poetry and short stories.

The two liberal newspapers *Dagbladet* and *Verdens Gang* were likewise organs for the new spirit of the times. From the close of the 70's, Georg Brandes was a regular contributor to the pages of *Dagbladet*.

During the period of literary flowering in the 80's, it is the positivistic view of life which is proclaimed in all the great writing, be it novels, plays or lyric poetry.

Bjørnson still appeared as a Grundtvigian Christian in 1876. However, his speech before the Students' Association the following year on the subject "Being in truth" marks the point where he parted company with Christian dogma. In lectures and articles during this and the following years, he rejected successively the doctrine of hell's punishment, the divinity of Christ, the atonement, and eternal life. His short story *Dust,* which in 1882 opened the first issue of *Nyt Tidsskrift,* was an attack on belief in immortality. The theory of evolution became his religion, and he proclaimed it in three poems titled *Hymns,* written in the late 70's.

Bjørnson next felt called upon to enlighten the Norwegian people on the results of scientific

Biblical criticism. He had ample opportunity for
this during several years' newspaper polemic, and
also published some pamphlets with this purpose
in mind. He seized upon the most radical works
on Biblical criticism he could find and either
translated them or popularized their ideas. In
1882 he published "From whence spring the miracles in the New Testament?" subtitled "chiefly
according to the third edition of Charles B.
Waite's *History of the Christian Religion.*" This
was a hypercritical and rather amateurish work
which Bjørnson had come across while on a lecture
tour to America a short time before. Christ's miracles and His resurrection must now be rejected,
declares Bjørnson in the foreword, since they are
"inventions from the second century without his-
toric basis."

In 1883 came the play *Beyond Human Power,* a
drama of purpose in which Bjørnson seeks to
prove the impossibility of Christianity. However,
as a drama of purpose it is weak, because the main
character, Pastor Sang, is pictured so beautifully
and the speeches about faith are so formed that
the effect can easily be the opposite of that
intended. That same year, however, Bjørnson
published another piece of propaganda with an
especially explicit message. He had made a translation of some articles by the American propa-

gandist for atheism, Robert Ingersoll, and had
titled them *Think for Yourself*. In the novel *On
the Paths of God* (1889), he effectively depicted
the spiritual clash of the age by aligning a Johnsonian pastor, representative of orthodox Christianity, against a physician, representative of the
new spirit.

Arne Garborg still appeared in 1876 as the
defender of orthodox Christianity, in a series of
newspaper articles in which he discussed the prob-
lem of religion. His religious temperament was
quite different from that of Bjørnson. He was
given to brooding and had gone far deeper into
Christianity. The strength of the anti-Christian
currents may be seen in his spiritual development.
Within just a few years, he swings over from being
spokesman for Church and Christianity to stand-
ing in the front rank of the opposition.

Garborg reviewed the position of Christianity
frankly in 1876, but still with confidence. It was
sorely threatened, but one should not be driven to
despair by the fact that politics, science, and cultural life are cutting themselves off from Christianity. For in this way religion is thrown back
into its proper sphere: the life of the individual.
"The Church now faces the task," he declared,
"of seeking to save practically an entire nation
from the final shipwreck of its faith." What is now

needed is "a serious, profound, and truth-loving sort of Christian apologetic" that can remove the new spirit's obstacles to faith without high-pressuring the mind or outwardly hindering unbelief. Youth can be won for the truth accordingly as "it manifests itself to them as truth"—or not. Above all, theology must have a clear understanding of "what stand it will take over against the natural sciences."

When, some years later, Norway found a defender of the faith of the type Garborg sought in Professor Fredrik Petersen, it was too late for Garborg. By that time he had broken with Christianity. Despite great vacillations in his religious views, he never returned to the faith of the church.

Garborg later stated that even as he was defending the faith in 1876, his faith had already been undermined. Bjørnson's speech in 1877 on "Being in truth" was the cause of his definitive break with Christianity. Garborg himself expressed his new views in a lecture before the Students' Association in 1881 on "The Principle of Religious Knowledge" and in his first novel *A Free-Thinker,* 1878. In the years that followed he subjected the apologetical works of the Norwegian theologians to a slashing criticism in *Nyt Tidsskrift.* He became the only one of the great poets openly to take exception also to the Christian morality and to advocate free love.

In the 1880's, Alexander Kielland brought out a series of elegantly written novels in which he never actually attacks Christianity, yet gives the church and its pastors a most merciless going over.

In the works of Ibsen, too, we can trace the pendulum's arc from a matter-of-course acceptance of Christian truths and norms in the 60's to the naturalism and skepticism of the 80's. *Brand,* which appeared in 1866, had the effect of an awakening proclamation of Christianity's claim on man. *Peer Gynt,* too, draws its main ideas from the Christian heritage. In *The Emperor and The Galilean,* Ibsen struggled with the idea of a synthesis of things human and things Christian into a higher unity—a third kingdom, formed by a union of the kingdoms of Christ and Caesar.

A new Henrik Ibsen greeted his readers in 1879, the author of *A Doll's House.* Then came *Ghosts, Enemy of the People, The Wild Duck,* and *Rosmersholm*—a series of heart-rending modern dramas pervaded by the spirit of pure skepticism and denial of all values. He speaks about the shams people cling to in order to go on living. The ethics of *A Doll's House* are clearly not Christian. When Christianity is mentioned at all in the dramas, the author's bent is unmistakable. Nora's

husband tries to detain her by appealing to morality and religion. She answers: "I know, of course,
only what Pastor Hansen said when I was prepar-
ing for confirmation . . . When I get away from all
this and find myself lonely, I will investigate that
matter, too . . . I will see whether what Pastor Hansen said was right, or at any rate, whether it was
right for *me*."

In *Ghosts* we meet an emancipated woman who
has made this investigation. Mrs. Alving says that
she had begun to examine the fabric of Pastor
Manders' teaching. "I was only going to pluck at
one single stitch; but when I had loosened that
one, the whole thing came unraveled. I realized
then that it had been machine-stitched."

It was in this atmosphere that the intellectually
alert people of the 1880's lived.

How deep did this de-Christianization go
among the people? How widespread was the wave
of secularization? Both Bjørnson and Garborg
thought that the entire nation was on the verge
of being swept away by it. This opinion was shared
by the theologian and folk high school leader
Christopher Bruun. He painted a gloomy picture
of the situation in 1884: "Free-thinking is sweep-
ing over students and educated youth like an
epidemic; it will soon seize the uneducated as
well." "The Church of this age is a church in

retreat." The Lord no longer marches with our armies. "We are losing one battle after another." The cause of it all is our apathetic Christianity, says repentance preacher Bruun. "The best we have to offer in a foundering Christianity."

The situation was not improved by the fact that the spiritual struggle of the 80's was intimately tied up with the political conflicts of that era. The struggle between the Conservative and the Liberal parties over the great issues of universal suffrage, power of the Storting as over against the Cabinet, and the royal veto in cases of Constitutional amendments, called forth political passions the like of which in modern times can only be found in the social struggles of the 1920's and the conflict between Norwegian patriots and the Nazis in the 1940's.

The Christians were engaged on both sides in the political battle. On the Liberal side were arrayed the Grundtvigians, but with them also a large share of the low-church, democratic revival groups, particularly in West Norway, together with the pastors who belonged to that wing. Most of the influential churchmen, however, allied themselves with the Conservatives. The very fact that the pastors were state officials gave them a natural place among the Conservatives. Moreover, there was in the Lutheran political ethos a tend-

ency toward conservatism which was clearly underscored in Gisle Johnson's lectures on ethics.
Finally, there was an obvious connection between
positivism and liberal politics. All of the positivists belonged to the political left. In conservative political circles, unbelief and political liberalism were thought to be cut from the same cloth.
They interpreted the contemporary political
struggle as one between the Christian principle of
authoritarianism and the rebellious, ungodly
principle of liberalism. "Only that spiritual trend
which knows nothing higher than the human will,
the spirit of unbelief, could hit upon the idea that
the right to vote is a (universal) human right,"
wrote J. C. Heuch.

In 1883, in a critical political situation, a sensational document titled *To Christianity's Friends
in Our Land* appeared in the conservative press.
It contained an appeal to all who desired the
preservation of Christianity in the land to witness
against unbelief and "the political movement
through which it seeks to gain its ends." Foremost
among its signers was Gisle Johnson. Each and
every bishop signed the document, five of the six
deans of the cathedrals, many well known clergymen, and many laymen, including a few of the
most famous lay-preachers. These men were to a
great extent representative of the church people.

The following year, 1884, the Conservatives suffered a decisive setback with the High Court of Justice decision and the introduction of the parliamentary system. "The Appealers," as the signers of the appeal were called by their opponents, had allied themselves with a lost cause.

The great and open falling-away provoked consternation in all Christian circles. In lay circles, which stood aloof from science and literature and therefore did not directly feel the pressure from the new spirit, the opinion was widespread that this unbelief was the beginning of the apostasy of the end times described in the Bible. There was a judgment-day mood in some of the preaching of the 80's, chiefly in the meeting houses and free-church gatherings. A series of books on the millennium and Christ's second coming saw the light of day. Needless to say, these books were read by quite another segment of the people than that which read Ibsen and *Nyt Tidsskrift*. There were also several attempts to calculate the exact time of Christ's return. With one exception, the clergy cautioned against these "pious fantasies," as Christopher Bruun called it. Church members among the educated classes saw clearly the need for an apologetic. And within a few years Norway acquired a whole apologetic literature.

J. C. Heuch was the first to feel called upon to defend the faith. He was in many ways well-suited to the task: His horizons had been widened by studies abroad, he was well-read, brilliant, and quick-witted. Beginning in 1876, he threw himself into the fight against unbelief with books, periodical articles and lectures. After the books *Modern Unbelief* (1876) and *Against Bjørnson's Attack on the Faith of the Christian Church* (1879) came his *magnum opus* in this field, *The Essence of Unbelief* (1883). The contents of this book are summed up in the two Scripture selections used as mottoes on the title-page: "If any man's will is to do His will, he shall know whether the teaching is from God," and Jesus' word to Jerusalem: " . . . But ye would not." The "essence" of unbelief is man's unwillingness to subject himself to God's authority. Heuch plays a number of variations on the main theme that unbelief has its roots in the will, not in the understanding. Science's objections to faith he treats very superficially. "It is not science, but this age's spirit of pride which inspires unbelieving men of science and engenders their opposition." He rejects all attempts to combine new scientific conclusions or new political concepts with Christianity: "A man should make up his mind either to believe in the dogmas of the modern mind [which he calls the dogmas of 'the right of the masses, culture's worldly bliss, and science's ability to determine what is truth in heaven as well as on earth'] and rely upon them in life and death, and so reject Christianity's dogmas, or have faith in Christianity and reject the claims of this age as untrue heathenism."

An entirely different note was struck by Professor Fredrik Petersen who had taken over the chair of Dogmatics at the University in 1875, and who created a stir in 1880 with his lecture on "How Ought the Church to Meet Contemporary Unbelief?" Unbelief, says this theologian, is rooted not only in the evil inclinations of the human heart but "it also meets an ideal need, a need for knowledge and progress." The Church must satisfy this need. It is the task of Christians to show "that Christianity is in no way inimical to the forward march of enlightenment. On the contrary, they are to prove that no one desires it more than Christendom." "They must then appropriate and incorporate into Christian thinking the results which contemporary scholarship has brought to light." Such incorporation of the results of modern scholarship will inevitably have great consequences for the Christian view of life. He says that "Christian thought and theology, once it has worked through these modern ideas, will undeniably appear entirely different from the older theology, hitherto ignorant of such ideas. We cannot avoid the conviction that this re-thinking is an imperative necessity."

With Fredrik Petersen's lecture in 1880 begins the history of modern theology in Norway. One of his critics immediately and quite correctly pointed out that Petersen's views approached those of the liberal Ritschlian school in Germany. In these two types of apologetic during the 80's, Heuch's and Petersen's, and in the incipient criticism of Petersen's viewpoint, we can discern the first germs of the strong tension between conservative and liberal theology that was to place its mark on Norwegian church life for the next fifty years.

During the 80's and 90's, Petersen wrote a number of books in which he attempted to realize his program. He was especially taken up with the relationship to the natural sciences. His main work is *Science and the Christian Faith* (1886), in which he confronts the Biblical creation narrative with natural science and discusses how belief in miracles and in God's answering prayer could be reconciled with the new perception of nature. In a series of books, he took up Positivism's objections to Christian morality, and attempted on the basis of

man's situations of choice and moral consciousness
to posit a religious and Christian way of life. His
distinction as an apologist lies in his willingness
and ability to see the matter also from the viewpoint of his opponents and to go into their arguments, and his readiness to admit mistakes on the
part of the church and defects in its understanding
of Christianity. He was firmly convinced that,
while theology was sometimes faulty, Christianity
itself need suffer no retrenchment whatever.

A little pamphlet by Petersen on the inspiration
of the Bible called forth polemic from the conservative camp because he made room for historical Bible research and was willing to yield to its
generally accepted results. In this struggle, Gisle
Johnson spoke out in defense of his colleague on
the faculty. Otherwise, Petersen had no one on the
faculty who shared his views until S. Michelet, A.
Brandrud, and Lyder Brun were appointed to
professorships in 1896 and 1897. These three
young theologians definitely belonged to the liberal school, though they represented it in a moderate and churchly form.

Petersen himself was radical in his principles,
but his opinions on the concrete dogmatic questions were conservative, and he specifically repudiated any attempt to criticize the doctrine of
the atonement. He was a transition theologian

who during his lifetime enjoyed the universal confidence also of the conservatives and who after his death was appropriated and quoted by both sides.

Petersen had like-minded friends among the clergy. His older contemporary, the philosophei and theologian Dr. E. F. B. Horn, who became pastor in the capital in 1882, had always been opposed to the reigning theology in Norway and came forward in the 80's and 90's as a spokesman for liberal views. Pastor J. J. Jansen, who had passed through a period of radical doubt in the late 70's, came out of his crisis with the frank belief that Christian truths could be reconciled with freedom of research and said so in fiery articles. The Grundtvigian Christopher Bruun began in 1884 to publish a periodical with the suggestive title *For Broadminded Christianity,* in which he attacked with equal vigor both free-thinkers and orthodox theologians and demanded a theology "which grasps the human element." Pastor Thorvald Klaveness had represented Johnsonian orthodoxy and pietism in the 70's. In 1875 he still saw no other means of correcting the anti-church tendencies of the day than to allow the judgment of God's Word to fall on everything which could conceivably draw people away from their childhood faith and to fight for Christian education in the schools in cooperation with the political Right. But already when he commented on Fredrik Petersen's lecture on the church and unbelief in the 1880's—Klaveness was then editor of *Luthersk Kirketidende*—a change had set in. Indeed, within the next few years he became a leading figure in the opposite camp—the anti-orthodox and anti-pietistic wing. When an old man, he told how the transition occurred gradually and without strong conflicts. His articles during the transition years bear out this statement. Yet the change he experienced was very great indeed. He had been struck by a remark made in the early 80's by the politically radical but dogmatically conservative Jakob Sverdrup that "present-day Christians are like people who stand on the river bank and lament the fact that the river flows by without stopping." Now he had awakened and had hurled himself out into the stream, and his program was "to bring the Christian elements into contact with cultural life and cultural life into contact with Christianity." He was joined in this aspiration by Christopher Bruun, and the two founded in 1893 the periodical *For Kirke og Kultur*, whose title contains its platform.

Klaveness' demand for a new preaching attracted great attention at the All-Lutheran Church

Conference at Lund in 1901. He told the delegates: "We must step down both from the cathedra of orthodox doctrine and from the pedestal of pietistic piety, and come into the midst of present-day mankind. We must sit down beside them with brotherly sympathy and listen to their thoughts and feelings. From this we must infer what they can accept of religious truth and how it must be proclaimed in order to be accepted . . . Brethren, I commend to you the modern cultural man."

Jansen's book *Everyday Sermons* (1891) had already introduced a new style of preaching: undogmatic, down-to-earth, and with an every-day vocabulary. Klaveness' sermon collection *The Gospel Proclaimed for the Present-Day* (1900) and Jansen's no less typical title *Place for Jesus* (1904) are outstanding examples of the new preaching, and they set the pattern for many others.

The new theology and the new preaching which emerged in the 90's called forth both concern and opposition from the conservative element. In inner mission circles there was considerable talk about the new rationalism which had infected several of the theological seminary teachers and leading pastors. In the church periodicals, a prolonged discussion was carried on with regard to Biblical criticism. Particularly untiring in his opposition to it was Pastor Storjohann, the father-in-law of liberal Professor Michelet.

After his appointment as Bishop of Christian-sand in 1889, J. C. Heuch had been relatively silent on matters of theological debate, except for a vehement dogmatic controversy in 1894 with one of the pastors in his diocese and a discussion with J. J. Jansen, who had called Harnack a rationalistic Christian—fully as absurd in Heuch's eyes as if he had called the man a Mohammedan Christian. Some of Klaveness' articles, however, caused him to take up the pen, and in 1902 he struck the modern theologians with a thunderbolt, in the form of a polemic book titled *Against the Stream*. This was a new "The Church's Reply," a document unparalleled in religious fervor, eloquent pathos, and demagogic appeal. He writes for the parishioner, and therefore translates his foreign words in the footnotes: "aristocracy" is rendered "society folks." "Oh, I know, all right, how people would have a man with my views to speak. How does today's theological jargon sound, again? Let me think a moment. Oh yes, for example, like this: 'In the joy with which we older people observe that the younger generation of theologians is able to combine scientific considerations with life there is, nevertheless, mingled with it a certain fear, which individual phenomena seem to confirm,

that people, in their efforts to give due considera-
tion to all factors, have perhaps not always avoided
giving the impression that they are approaching
a somewhat too rationalistic interpretation of
Christianity. However, when one looks at the
names of the leading theologians, who vouch for
the fact that in this case science and piety go hand
in hand, every such fear is easily dispelled.' Isn't
it so? When I write like that, I am a good boy who
understands his age and, even though he is 'against
the stream' in his heart, still quite genially allows
himself to be swept along by it.

"But if I could write thus, I would not have
written. For then these things would not possess
so much interest for me that I would expose myself to all the unpleasantness of sharp polemic.
For years I have kept silent. Every new message
from Christiania, every meeting I heard about,
every theological volume I read offended me in-
creasingly. I have often felt as though I were in-
haling impure air. I noticed that a poison began
to filter in here and there among the teachers and
pastors. Still I kept quiet. I was too old and tired
to go to war. But then, this fall came that lecture
at Lund, with its open and haughty unfurling of
the banner of Transition Theology. This was followed by the diocesan meeting in Christiania,
with its farce on the menace of rationalism . . .

while those from whose quarter it threatened
either were, or with the greatest of ease could have
been, present in the hall . . . When I saw that
scandalous spectacle, I could no longer hold my
peace . . .

"A stream which carries with it the vast majority of those who seem to be distinguished by learning, ability, indeed even piety, appears difficult to
stop. At any rate, I know very well that this book
will not be able to stem the tide any more than a
chip can dam up a raging torrent. But the Lord
in heaven can say to the stream: 'Turn around.
Be still, proud waves.' And that great multitude
which the Lord still has in our country will assemble in concerted prayer that the Lord will
allow us to behold the Gospel's light and make the
mists of human teaching to lift. If I could make
the living congregation see what danger we find
ourselves in, so that the congregation would
awaken to vigilance and prayer and less easily
allow themselves to be taken captive by beautiful
phrases, then my work will not have been in vain."

Heuch's appeal to the congregation was not in
vain. Coming events were to reveal that.

In 1903, Fredrik Petersen died. One of the two
applicants for the vacant chair was Johannes
Ording, a theologian of decidedly liberal views.
A selection committee of experts found his com-

petitor incompetent and declared that Ording indeed possessed the academic qualifications, but
that in his view of the sacraments he was outside
the "the confessional basis" that must be present
in the Theological Faculty's instruction, and therefore he could not be recommended for the position. The faculty's liberal majority did not share
this opinion, and nominated Ording for appointment, while its lone conservative member, Professor S. Odland, dissented. Odland warned the Minister for Church Affairs that Ording's appointment would have the most catastrophic consequences for the church, and the Ministry received
petitions from the bishops, from the Christiania
Pastoral Association, from the Board of the Inner
Mission Society *(Indremissionsselskabet)*, and
from a number of local inner mission groups,
protesting against the appointment of a man who
stood in open conflict with the church's confession. The Government then decided, with some
dissenting votes, not to appoint Ording.

In 1904, the professorship in systematic theology
was again declared open, this time for Scandinavi-
an competition. Five of the six foreign judges
placed Dr. Ording at the head of the list, and the
faculty nominated him to the post, Odland again
dissenting. The Minister for Church Affairs tried
in a number of ways to get around appointing

Ording but was voted down by his fellow cabinet members, and Johannes Ording was appointed professor of theology on January 27, 1906.

Both sides attached the deepest, most fundamental importance to the conflict over Ording's appointment. For Ording and the faculty majority it was a matter of safeguarding academic freedom, while the feeling was strong in the church that Ording's appointment represented a violation of the church's confessional character.

The appointment of Ording had far-reaching consequences for the history of the church in Norway. Professor Odland immediately tendered his resignation. The Minister for Church Affairs, Christoffer Knudsen, had already resigned (and his resignation had been accepted) at the cabinet meeting which appointed Ording. He now became the leading figure in a committee gathering funds to enable Professor Odland to lecture outside the University. The idea of establishing a free theological faculty soon emerged, and Odland named it *Menighetsfakultetet* (The Congregation's Faculty). An appeal to the church people requesting support for the proposed theological school was signed by two of the bishops and a number of well-known pastors and laymen. *Menighetsfakultetet* was able to begin its work in the fall of 1908, for the time being without the right of examination. This right was granted by the Storting in 1913.

With the establishment of Menighetsfakultetet, an old tension within the church had found institutional expression. The tension between Haugeans and clergy, between "scriptural theologians" and Grundtvigians, and between the spiritual trends represented by Heuch and Fredrik Petersen had led to an institutional split which in time was to encompass other matters as well. And with it, the framework for twentieth century Norwegian church life was drawn up.

Chapter Four

Conflicts of the Twentieth Century:
Victory for the Lay Movement
Dissension Within the Church
Churchly Appeasement

The first half of the twentieth century is the time of victory for the organized lay-movement in the Norwegian Church.

The Conventicle Act was repealed in 1842. In the 1880's lay preaching was recognized as legitimate by the church; Augustana Article 14 was waived. All lay-preaching had to take place outside the churches until Jakob Sverdrup in 1888 obtained the royal decree which permitted lay-preachers to speak in the churches, although not yet from the pulpits. In 1913 the Storting revoked the legal provision prohibiting laymen from preaching at the regular Sunday services. Since then, lay-preaching at Sunday services by travelling secretaries and emissaries of the various Christian organizations, with the pastor in the pew, has become a not uncommon phenomenon.

In 1891 *Lutherstiftelsen* gave up its "Emergency Principle" and reorganized under the name *Det norske lutherske Indremissionsselskab*. When friends of inner mission united to form one nation-wide organization in 1893, one of the speakers correctly appraised the significance of that event: "We know that from this time forward the Norwegian Inner Mission will stand as one united power, whose influence will soon be felt in wide circles."

In the original statutes of *Indremissionsselskabet* from the year 1893, its relation to the ecclesiastical establishment is characterized as follows: "In all its activity the association will, in so far as practicable, seek to work in conjunction with the ministerial office."

Efforts for a union of all inner mission friends at the opening of the 90's had, meanwhile, met with determined opposition in West Norway. A series of great revivals had passed through the districts there during the 70's and 80's and both the awakened laymen and their pastors had adopted a critical attitude toward the church. The westerners demanded a completely free Inner Mission and were willing to cooperate with pastors of their own stripe, but only because they were of the right viewpoint, not because they were pastors. The net result was the establishment in 1898 of a separate West Norway Inner Mission Alliance *(Det Vestlandske Indremisjonsforbund)* with head quarters in Bergen.

Whereas *Indremissionsselskapet* had stated that it would "seek to work in conjunction with the ministerial office," *Det Vestlandske Indremisjons-forbund* expressed its relation to the church as follows: "The Alliance will, as far as possible in its activity, place itself in support of and cooperation with holders of the churchly office." The difference in wording is minor, but it is characteristic. It expresses a difference in spirit which is so great that later attempts to merge the two large home mission organizations have been frustrated and finally given up completely. It did not even help when *Indremissionsselskapet* in 1914 deleted the word "office" from its laws—partly to approach the westerners, partly because the office could, of course, be held by liberal theologians—and said that the Association would work in brotherly un- derstanding "with our congregations' other Chris- tian agencies which stand on the foundation of God's Word and our church's confessions." What still stood between them was the fact that *Indre- missionsselskapet* still followed the principles laid down by Hans Nielsen Hauge and desired its members to attend the church's worship services and to "receive the sacraments" from its pastors, while *Vestlandske Indremisjonsforbund* did not hesitate to set its meetings up as a substitute for the state church service, and both in principle and often also in practice preferred to celebrate Holy Communion within its own group, administered by a layman.

In the meantime, there arose another Christian organization which was to become still more radical in its criticism of the church than the *Vestlandske* group. This new union was formed at a meeting of missions-minded people at Bergen in 1890 and soon adopted the name *Det norske Lutherske Chinamissionsforbund* ("The Norwegian Lutheran China-Mission Alliance"). Since 1949 it has been called *Norsk Luthersk Misjonssamband.*

This competitor to the then fifty-year old and very active *Norske Misjonsselskap* (Norwegian Missionary Society) was brought into being partly out of interest in China, a mission field that NMS was very hesitant about tackling, and partly out of dissatisfaction over the policy toward the church which the older missionary society was following. This latter motive had substantial significance and stood in the way of all NMS' subsequent efforts toward a union of the two.

From the very beginning, many of *Chinafor-*

bundet's members were free-churchly out of principle, holding that the ecclesiastical ordinances were un-Biblical. Within a few years, they simply established themselves as a sort of free church within the state church. Both their own ideals and the distrust they met from the side of the church drove them in that direction. When three bishops refused their request for ordination of their first missionary, he went to China without ordination, and soon after, the general assembly of the Alliance resolved that its missionaries would in future be ordained by the Alliance's director in a public act of ordination. The clerical gown was not to be worn on the mission field, and the service was to have a very simple liturgy without any formal prayers. Communion was to be received sitting down, the participants themselves passing around the bread and wine.

A corresponding form for celebrating Communion was soon introduced also in the homeland. Some lay-preachers from *Chinaforbundet* and *Vestlandske Forbundet* began in 1906 to advocate what they called free Communion, without an ordained pastor, administered among the inner circle of believers.

The lay-preachers' *Vestlandske Broderring* demanded the "emancipation of Holy Communion," that is, repeal of the ban on private celebration of

Communion which still stood in the law-books.
A number of ecclesiastical authorities expressed
themselves as favoring abolition of the civil law's
old punishment for private Communion: It was
incompatible with religious freedom. The Storting accordingly repealed these provisions in 1913.
The decision was hailed with great joy by the
westerners and the people of *Chinaforbundet.*
Holy Communion had now been "freed," according to their conception, just as the preaching of
the Word had been freed by repeal of the Conventicle Act in 1842.

On the other hand, they evinced little enthu-
siasm for a royal decree of 1913 which attempted
to render private Communion compatible with
the Church's principles by authorizing the bishops
to commission those laymen who were to admin-
ister Communion. Lay administrators commissioned by the bishops were precisely what they did
not want. As a result, this regulation had absolute-
ly no practical significance, for since 1913 singular-
ly few have been commissioned, and those few
who have been have had little to do.

In spite of all its opposition to church order,
the radical lay movement nevertheless considered
itself Lutheran and always called itself by that
name. Moreover, its adherents had no desire to
leave the state church. At the same time, they re-

garded the state church congregations as mission fields. Their leading church politician, Ludvig Hope, has firmly upheld the state church as an arrangement pedagogically useful for the people and one which prepares a favorable mission field. The state church is "a scaffold we stand on to build the Church of Jesus Christ." Thus, a positive evaluation of the state church was possible also from this viewpoint.

Beginning in the mid-90's the Christian organizations experienced a rapid growth. Within a couple of decades, each of the three large organizations had hundreds of local associations throughout the country *(Indremissionsselskapet* had 950 in 1912) and hundreds of itinerant preachers *(Chinaforbundet* alone had 300 in 1912). This growth has continued, though at a slower rate. *Vestlandske Indremisjonsforbund's* field of operations has always been almost exclusively in West Norway. *Chinamisjonsforbundet,* on the other hand, became firmly established in East Norway as well, and eventually moved its headquarters and its school to Oslo in 1912.

Lay activity changed character under this type of organization. The first permanent preachers' school was opened in Bergen in 1888. Later, all the large organizations founded their own Bible schools and youth schools. Furthermore, they had

their own periodicals, and acquired their own
publishers and printers. The management of
hotels became one of their specialties—undoubtedly patterned after the Danish Inner Mission. The
phenomenal growth of the work is illustrated by
the fact that, during the thirty-three years Pastor
Johan Martin Wisløff was general secretary of
Indremissionsselskapet (1912-44), its organ *For
Fattig og Rik* (For Poor and Rich) increased its
circulation from 2,500 to 55,000. Wisløff super-
vised the building of ten to twelve youth schools,
a Bible school in Oslo, a Christian high school, a
Christian agricultural school, and two Christian
teachers' colleges, of which *Indremissionen* gave
up one and was deprived of the other when the
state in 1946 demanded control of the Oslo teachers' college. In addition, the organizations received
their own theological faculty—for *Menighetsfakultetet* has, to a large extent though not exclusively,
received its economic support and recruited its
students from the Christian milieu of these organizations.

Some degree of inter-organizational cooperation
also came into being once the expansion period
was over and the proportional numerical strength
of the organizations stabilized. Since 1912, annual
nation-wide rallies have been held, at which Inner
Mission supporters of all shades of opinion gather

for edifying meetings lasting several days, while debatable points are excluded. In 1916, these rallies were also thrown open to members of dissenting bodies, but this decision was revoked shortly after the Second World War, as a result of an increasing Lutheran confessionalism. In 1913, leaders from all the large Christian organizations met with representatives for seamen's missions, youth work, Sunday schools, etc. Geilo, lying halfway between east and west Norway, was chosen as the site for the meeting. The Geilo meetings became a perennial institution until 1937, when they were superseded by a permanent cooperating committee called *Organisasjonenes Fellesraad* (O.F.) which consists of the general secretaries of the various organizations, and thus forms a kind of collegium of unordained bishops. The cooperation of the big organizations has, however, undergone several severe tests, and in 1917, *China-misjonsforbundet* withdrew from the Geilo meetings and has since declined membership in O.F.

Within the space of one century, Hauge's little flocks had thus become—in keeping with the democratic development of the age and what has been called its "association tendency"—powerful organizations complete with a press, schools, and huge administrative staffs. But the spontaneity of the movement has disappeared. Since the end of the

1920's constant complaint over the mutual competition, over-organization, and stagnation has
been voiced by the organizations' own men. They
continue to scan the horizon for awakenings. But
the awakening stage seems to have been replaced
by that of organization.

The struggle between the two theological
trends within the Norwegian Church had become
acute when a professor was to be appointed to suc-
ceed the late Fredrik Petersen. With the opening
of *Menighetsfakultetet* in 1908, it became chronic.
At the time, *Menighetsfakultetet* was viewed as
a temporary institution. Its promoters looked forward to the day when the church people could
once again safely entrust the training of their pastors to the University's theological faculty.

That day has not yet arrived. On the contrary,
Menighetsfakultetet has experienced a vigorous
growth. In the beginning, the student body was
small, and there was a serious crisis when Professor Odland in 1916 left the faculty he had
founded. His conscience would not allow him to
remain as theological professor in a church which
had given women the right to speak in the
churches. But by that time, *Menighetsfakultetet*
had discovered a new leader in his younger colleague Ole Hallesby, a man who was soon to dis-

play great leadership ability in the church struggle. The student body grew during the 1920's, so that it soon exceeded that of the University faculty. The position of *Menighetsfakultetet* in the church was also fortified by a large number of supporting groups and fund-gathering committees, by regular offerings in the churches, and by travelling secretaries who pleaded the institution's cause before the church people.

Beginning with the "professor struggle," an impassioned exchange of words continued between liberal and conservative theologians for a quarter of a century. The liberals founded *Norsk Kirkeblad* in 1904 as their organ, while the old *Luthersk Kirketidende* represented the right wing. These two periodicals carried on a debate for fully two decades, with many people participating in the often sharp commentary. This was supplemented by a deluge of books and pamphlets and not least newspaper articles, particularly when the situation became acute due to some "incident" or another.

One such episode was the Konow case. Resident Curate Carl Konow delivered some public lectures at Bergen in 1906 and 1907 in which he rejected the Virgin Birth and Jesus' pre-existence and bodily resurrection and advocated rather extreme views of Biblical criticism. A pastoral conference in Bergen voted unanimously to request Konow's resignation. The Minister for Church Affairs also approached him with a similar suggestion, but Konow was adamant. Since the Ministry was unwilling to bring legal action against him, he remained in his position, but a *modus vivendi* was found, an additional pastor was appointed to his congregation.

The liberal pastors organized themselves in 1913 into a group called "The Progressive Norwegian Ministerial Group." In 1919 the conservatives established their "Brotherhood of Pastors Loyal to the Church's Confession."

The conservatives made use of old Grundtvigian formulas. They battled for "the faith of the congregation," and the Apostles' Creed was pushed into the foreground. The conservative wing, as it was represented by the clergy and *Menighetsfakultetet,* was definitely not fundamentalist—undoubtedly to the disappointment of some of the lay people who had hoped that *Menighetsfakultetet* would be a preachers' school that was faithful to the Bible. The conservatives used the Apostles' Creed as a summary of what Christianity is, and it is suggestive that the Old Grundtvigian Christopher Bruun, who had demanded a new theology in the 90's, toward the end of his life, vehemently objected to the "undermining

work" of the liberals and said that "The only
right thing to do is to meet it with Dr. Hallesby's
stormy declaration of war." The parallel between
the conservatives' fight and that of Grundtvig in
"The Church's Reply" was underscored in a little book by Olaf Moe in 1925, the centennial
year of Grundtvig's battle-cry.

In 1919 Edvard Sverdrup, professor at *Menighetsfakultetet* and president of *Indremissionsselskapet,* offered the liberals a truce, provided they
would accept the Apostles' Creed "word for word,"
an offer which was rejected by Professor Lyder
Brun, who said that the liberals "refuse, as historically thinking evangelical Christians, to iden-
tify faith with a fixed complex of historically conditioned sentences." The battle-cry "Confessional
Fidelity" referred chiefly to the Apostles' Creed
during the first decades of the church struggle,
while the specific Lutheran confessions have come
to the fore in later years.

The theologians' discussions were followed with
the most vivid interest by the common people.
The fight became bitter and personal, and the
gulf widened steadily. Just how deep it went was
to be revealed in connection with an irenic church
rally held at Drammen in September 1919, where
men from both camps sat side by side and spoke
together as brothers. The chairman of the arrange-

ments committee was the conservative but peace-
able Bishop Jens Tandberg who thought that,
commensurate with the ecumenical movement
then in its embryonic stage, the hand of brotherhood ought to be extended also to the liberals
at home. Both liberals and conservatives sat on
the committee, but when Professor Hallesby violently attacked the project in the newspapers, all
the conservatives either withdrew or declared that
they had not intended a cooperation which involved recognition of the liberals. Only Bishop
Tandberg stood his ground. He neither retracted
nor modified his viewpoint. The Bishop was at
the time chairman of the board of directors of
Menighetsfakultetet, but was not reelected in the
fall of 1919 and was forced to bow out. The
general convention of the Norwegian Pastors'
Association that same autumn was unusually tur-
bulent. One of the speakers characterized the
University's theological school as an "immense in-
justice against the congregations."

At the proposal of Hallesby, the Geilo meeting's continuation committee decided to hold a
big national meeting in Christiania because of the
church situation. This meeting took place in the
Calmeyer Street mission house, February 15-18,
1920. It was a conclave of that whole segment of
the Norwegian Church which belonged to the

organizations. Invitations were sent out to the various Christian organizations within the church, and the 950 participants were representatives chosen by their organizations. The assembly adopted a resolution renouncing any and all co-operation with the liberals. Where congregations had liberal pastors, "we assert the right of the living congregation to make use of God's Word, Baptism, and Holy Communion in other legal ways." Indicative of the meeting's spirit is the fact that a separate vote was taken over whether the word "legal" should be included. It was up-held against a strong minority.

The 1920's were years of discord in all spheres of life. Fanned by strikes and unemployment the political antagonism reached an intensity equal to that of the 1880's; it was the bourgeoisie against the labor movement, the social democrats against the communists. Attempts to force an armed class struggle entered the picture. Among leading fig-ures in the Labor Party there was marked animos-ity toward the church. And within the church, tension between the liberals and the conservatives reached its peak. The tone of theological debate became if possible even more bitter than during the sharpest attacks on the Grundtvigians in the preceding century.

In 1923, the Government appointed the liberal

Dr. Theol. Jens Gleditsch to the vacant Nidaros bishopric with the express motive that the liberals too ought to have a representative in the college of bishops. His appointment greatly offended the conservatives, partly because Gleditsch had been a sharp and ironic polemicist, and partly because he had received far fewer votes in the balloting than his conservative opponent. Parish councils had been introduced in the Norwegian Church in 1920, and the first two bishops appointed by the Government after 1920 had been the candidates proposed by the councils. In this case, it was expected that the bishops would refuse to ordain Gleditsch. Most of them, led by the Bishop of Oslo, Johan Lunde, were indeed unwilling to carry out the ordination. The irenic Bishop Bernt Støylen of Christiansand, however, relieved the situation by ordaining Gleditsch, after first conferring with him and assuring himself that Gleditsch shared the church's faith. Støylen, however, had in this matter acted contrary to the mandate of the Calmeyer Street meeting, thus alienating himself, even though he personally was conservative. Missions-minded people in Christiansand, however, lacked the sharp sense for drawing clear lines which the lay leaders had. A couple of years later, they arranged a missions rally at which they wanted both their bishop and Dr. Hallesby to speak. Hallesby publicly stated that he could not participate in any cooperative endeavor with Bishop Støylen in view of the fact that he had ordained Gleditsch.

Both the liberal and the conservative wings embraced moderates as well as extremists. Johannes Ording was stubborn by nature and the treatment he had received made him more radical in the days following the professor struggle. Several times he defied the church people with his statements. He stood definitely to the left of his faculty colleague Lyder Brun, who took express exception to some of Ording's views. In the 1920's the most extreme liberal theology was expressed by the young Kristian Schjelderup, doctor of theology, assistant lecturer in theology at the University from 1921-1927. He gave up historical Christianity and sought refuge in general religion. He took a study tour to the Far East to acquaint himself with Buddhism and subsequently published (1923) a travel description, *Where Men Become Gods,* marked by a strong sympathy for the religions of the East. In 1924 he provoked the moderate liberals in a series of newspaper articles in which he taunted them with charges of indecision and dishonesty in their half-way measures. These articles were published in book form under the title *Who Jesus Was and What the Church Has Made of Him.* Here, every basis for a

Christology or a religious relation to the Person of Christ was swept aside. Jesus was simply a religious genius and a man who could lead many people in the world of religion. The book touched off a violent feud in the press, where the liberals turned their guns on Schjelderup, while the leading conservatives agreed with him in his criticism of the liberals and with satisfaction pointed out what liberal theology led to.

In 1928, Dr. Schjelderup made application for the vacant pastorate in Vaerøy and Røst parish. The situation was dramatic. It was one of the least attractive calls in the country, extremely lonely and exposed to the rigors of climate, and the controversial and also somewhat feted doctor of theology was the only applicant. The Minister for Church Affairs did not refer the matter to any ecclesiastical authority, but declared summarily that Dr. Schjelderup could not be appointed to any pastorate because of his attitude to the church's confession. The Government sided with him. A liberal politician questioned the decision in the Storting and the Labor Party attempted to override the Government, but failed to gain a majority vote.

In the 1920's, the institutional cleavage begun by the founding of *Menighetsfakultetet* was extended. In 1924, Kristian Schjelderup was reelected to the presidency of *Norske Studenters Kristelige Forbund,* just at the time when his challenges were most defiant. The more orthodox students had for some time had little to do with *Studenterforbundet* and had been holding their own summer meetings instead. Now they attempted to win the presidency with Professor Hallesby as their candidate. When the attempt failed, they walked out and established in the spring of 1924 *Norges Kristelige Studentlag,* an organization that was soon destined to have far more members than *Kristelige Studenterforbund* and which later extended its activities to include the high schools.

In 1925 *Menighetsfakultetet* opened its own Practical Theological Seminary, and in 1929 started its own periodical, *Tidsskrift for Teologi og Kirke.* The State's Practical Seminary had been headed, during the acute years of the conflict, by a markedly liberal rector, whose appointment in 1916 meant the passing up of a very competent conservative theologian. And *Norsk Teologisk Tidsskrift* must have long been a thorn in the side of the conservatives, particularly because of its annual surveys of Norwegian church life, which the editors never entrusted to any but the most confirmed liberals. The liberals, shunned by the entire organized Christian front, under Lyder

Brun's leadership, held fast to the positions they possessed, and utilized them to the fullest, without concessions to the other wing, and without much psychology. The net result was that the conservatives established new institutions and the institutional split was complete.

After the tempestuous 1920's, the 30's were remarkably peaceful. Even as early as the 900-years' jubilee of the battle of Stiklestad in 1930, the great national church festivities were held without incident. And the ensuing years were peaceful.

This turnabout was undoubtedly conditioned by the fact that the spirit of the times changed both at home and abroad, and that new theological trends reached Norway. Even after the middle of the 1920's theological literature appeared in Norway which knew no other alternative than liberal or conservative, as for example Professor S. Michelet's book *Christianity and Rationalism* (1927). But about 1930, new tones filtered into the debate, influenced by the dialectical theology and other Continental trends which were instrumental in tempering the old party strife.

A kind of weariness, a longing for peace, was also in evidence. The Progressive Norwegian Ministerial Group disbanded in 1928. That same year, Schjelderup founded a "National Associa-

tion for Broad-minded Christianity," to include
liberal laymen as well as pastors, but his followers
were very few. The National Association was dis-
solved in 1933 and its periodical failed.

The 1930's were destitute of dramatic events.
Instead, a quiet growth in churchliness took place
which was especially discernible in the steady rise
in the number of communicants. Thus, there was
a recurrence of what had happened a century
earlier: Under the influence of a more conservative and churchly spirit, an entire generation of
liberal clergymen modified their views almost im-
perceptibly, while younger men who had not lived
through the most bitter phase of the church struggle gave more confident expression to the new
orthodoxy of the day.

In 1934, the Oxford Group Movement reached
Norway and had a most beneficial effect on the
church life. In Norway the relations between the
Groups and the Church became more intimate
than in other European countries. Men like the
author Ronald Fangen and the journalist Fredrik
Ramm, who were deeply rooted in the heritage of
their church, became leaders of the movement,
and many pastors joined the Groups. People who
were converted normally became church-goers and
communicants.

That complete peace in the church had not

been achieved came to light when Eivind Berggrav, doctor of theology, was transferred in 1937
from the bishopric of Haalogaland to that of Oslo.
Professor Hallesby wrote in a newspaper that he
could not welcome Berggrav to Oslo unless he re-
nounced his liberal past and unreservedly took
a stand on the confession of the church. "Until
that happens, we will pray."

This time, the interdict had no effect. The
experience of the Middle Ages—that when the ban
has been used too often and is applied in a situation where it lacks the support of popular opinion, it is null and void—was repeated. Berggrav
had received an overwhelming majority of votes
in parish councils of the Oslo diocese and was
met with confidence everywhere.

The 1940's were rich in dramatic events. In
the church's fight against Nazism occasioned by
the German occupation of Norway, the leadership
fell to Berggrav both on account of his position
and on the strength of his personality.

Berggrav had early become convinced that if
the church should ever face a critical situation,
cooperation between the bishops and the Christian organizations would have to be established.
He had put forth this idea at a meeting of the
bishops as early at 1930, when the then particular-

ly unfriendly Labor Party was likely to gain a majority in the Storting. The idea met with little sympathy among his colleagues. But when the Second World War broke out, even before Norway became involved, he was working to consolidate the Christian front. In September 1939 he succeeded in getting Hallesby to sign with him an appeal to Norway's Christians for confidence and prayer.

During the summer and fall of 1940, an important consolidation of the Christian front was carried out, on the initiative of Berggrav. At a meeting in his home on October 25, a permanent group calling itself "Joint Christian Council for the Norwegian Church" was formed. It consisted of, among others, Bishop Berggrav, Professor Ole Hallesby, and lay-preacher Ludvig Hope, the "grand old man" of *Chinamisjonsforbundet,* a man who throughout a long life had consistently opposed the clergy. He and Berggrav had met one another for the first time as late as 1939. They represented two sides of the Norwegian Church between which there had not been much contact.

On October 28, 1940, the Joint Christian Council made a public appearance at a meeting in Calmeyer Street mission house, where Bishops Berggrav and Støren and lay-leaders Hallesby and Hope spoke. A declaration was read in which the

Joint Council pledged that it would "Follow without circumlocution our old, tested Reformation and Haugean lines, on the basis of the inspired Word of God as interpreted in our church's Lutheran confessions."

Some press comment on the happy situation that conservatives and liberals now stood together in the Joint Christian Council gave rise to a further statement of its basis by the Council; it was "Biblical, Lutheran, and Haugean." "If men or movements must, in future, arise to tear our Bible to pieces, deny that Jesus Christ was conceived by the Holy Ghost and born of the Virgin Mary, make Jesus' Cross a martyr's cross and deny His atoning death and bodily resurrection, the Joint Christian Council certainly will not shrink from a battle for the true faith." This declaration, together with an assurance that the intention was not to place the organizations under church leadership, demonstrates how difficult it was to assemble a Christian front.

Yet consolidation succeeded, and it was precisely this consolidation which made the church's fight possible. High points in the struggle were the Bishops' pastoral letter on the church and the legal system (February 1941), also signed by the leaders of the Christian organizations; resignation of the bishops on February 24, 1942; resignation of the pastors at Easter of the same year, motivated by the confessional document "Basis of the Church"; establishment of a "Temporary Church Council" in the summer of 1942; and the open statements of this council against persecution of the Jews and conscription for war purposes of Norwegian citizens in violation of international law. These events are well known and will therefore not be commented upon here.

Concord lasted also for some time after the war and found expression in, among other things, the strong wave of sentiment which swept the controversial Kristian Schjelderup into the office of Bishop of Hamar. He had occupied himself in the 30's with problems of spiritual freedom, had evidently at that time no positive interest in the church, and in 1938 founded the Nansen School, a folk high school on a common cultural, humanistic basis. During the fall of 1940 he experienced a religious break-through, and served as preacher and pastor for his fellow-prisoners at Grini concentration camp. After the war, he was warmly accepted in all circles within the church. His career advanced rapidly: Assistant pastor in 1945, resident curate in our Savior's Church, Oslo, in 1946, and in 1947, Bishop of Hamar.

We now stand at the end of a period in Norwegian Church History which will in the future perhaps be called the Berggrav epoch. He is the central figure of both the 30's and the 40's, flanked by important churchmen like Hallesby and Hope. He is interesting as a liberal churchman who in the 1920's and 30's oriented himself in a positive churchly direction. But he is an especially interesting figure in his capacity as the rallying point in the church's struggle during the occupation and will be remembered for his leadership, which surely is not lacking in greatness.

We have carried church history right up to the present day, to the point where history gives way to journalism. A historian would have preferred stopping a bit earlier, at a point where the source material is more surveyable and somewhat more worked over, where the historical perspective is greater, and where he is not himself engaged in the events occurring. Yet men like Eusebius, Vincent de Beauvais, and Gilbert Burnet carried church history right up to their own day. In so doing, one not only has their example with which to excuse oneself, but one can attempt to interpret the signs of one's own time through an understanding of what the preceding generation sought, the problems it faced, and the decisions it took. Thus ought church history to be made to serve the life of the church today.

INDEX